INC
Sights

A Teacher's
Guide to
Writers
INC

A few words about *INC Sights* . . .

The *INC Sights* you are now reading reflects the latest thinking on a number of writing-related issues. It was compiled as a general "guidebook" to our *Writers INC* handbook and will . . .

- introduce you to the handbook,
- discuss approaches for incorporating *Writers INC* into your classroom (and across the curriculum),
- supply you with minilessons, scavenger hunts, and other activities for daily writing and language practice, and
- provide a close-up look at the *Writers File*, our coordinating 9-12 writing program.

We are genuinely enthused about our *INC Sights*, just as we are about the handbook itself. We hope that after you've seen our materials close up, you'll share our enthusiasm. If you have any questions, suggestions, or observations, please let us know. We'd love to hear from you.

Third Edition ■ First Printing
ISBN 0-939045-82-6

Contents

- What is *Writers INC?*
- What are the contents?
- How is the handbook arranged?

The opening section of *INC Sights* provides an overview of both the content and style of the handbook.

- Section Samplers
- Popular Spots

The "tour" includes a preview of actual pages and a list of specific features ("Popular Spots") within each section in *Writers INC.*

- Where does *Writers INC* fit in?
- Using the Handbook

Two important features here include a "cluster" of ideas for using *Writers INC* and a series of getting-started activities that will help teachers introduce students to the handbook. Reproducible activities are included.

- Contemporary Writing Programs
- Setting Up a Schoolwide Writing Program
- Planning Writing Assignments
- Implementing an Experience-Based Writing Program
- Implementing a Writing Workshop
- Evaluating Student Writing
- Using Writing Portfolios
- What about Grammar?

An overview of contemporary writing programs introduces this section. Also included is a suggested framework of writing activities for grades 9-12 and suggestions for implementing a writing workshop. Of special interest will be the information on responding to and evaluating writing and using writing portfolios.

A Writers INC: An Overview

What is *Writers INC?*

Writers INC is our popular writing, thinking, and learning handbook designed with today's secondary students in mind. Its appealing personality and wealth of information set it apart from any other handbook now in use. (In a November 1991 article in the ***English Journal***, *Writers INC* received more recommendations from teachers than any other handbook. (See pp. 30-31 in this booklet for a copy of the article.)

How can *Writers INC* be used in high school?

Primary Text • *Writers INC* can be used as the primary resource for writing and language learning *for all students in grades 9-12*. Teachers can use it as a teaching text to initiate writing and learning. Students can use it as a reference book when they are working on the activities in the *Writers File* series or when they are working on other writing and learning projects.

All-School Handbook • *Writers INC* also works well as an all-school handbook. (In fact, this is how it works best.) Because it is portable, user-friendly, and comprehensive, students will find it an invaluable resource not only in their English classes, but also across the curriculum. (See "Writing to Learn," pp. 70-75.)

Self-Improvement Book • A handbook as appealing and friendly as *Writers INC* makes a perfect guide for improving writing and learning skills. It has that special quality Thomas Carlyle said all good books should have: the ability to "excite a reader into self-activity."

What are the key sections in *Writers INC?*

Writers INC is divided into eight major sections, each dealing with a key area of writing and language learning:

The Writing Process • Special attention is given to prewriting and revising—two critical steps in the development of meaningful writing.

Style & Form • Advice and insights are provided for writers who are genuinely concerned about improving their writing style. Also offered here are guidelines for writing paragraphs and essays.

Searching & Researching • Steps in the research process are clearly and thoroughly described. Example parenthetical references and bibliographic entries are given for both the MLA and APA styles.

Special Forms of Writing • Poetry, the short story, newswriting, writing about literature, and business writing (including résumés) are addressed in this section.

Reading & Learning • Everything from improving reading and note-taking skills to test-taking and college-prep skills is covered here.

Speaking & Thinking • Special emphasis is given to formal speaking and to thinking creatively and logically.

Final Re-marks: A Proofreader's Guide This handbook within a handbook answers any questions a writer might have concerning punctuation, grammar, usage, and mechanics.

Appendix • The full-color maps, historical documents, helpful conversion charts, and other useful lists included here make *Writers INC* well suited for schoolwide use.

What are the contents of each *Writers INC* section?

■ Personal Writing | The opening essay invites and challenges students to engage in personal writing so as to learn more about themselves and their world, and the craft of writing.

The Writing Process

■ Using the Writing Process
■ Writing Guidelines

In "The Writing Process" students are introduced to writing as a process of exploration and discovery rather than an end product. "Writing Guidelines" includes a summary of the steps in the writing process, guidelines for selecting and shaping a writing idea, a useful list of writing topics, and a survey of writing forms.

Style & Form

■ Writing with Style
■ Writing Paragraphs
■ Writing Essays

"Writing with Style" first addresses the traits of effective writing and then examines common stylistic "ailments." Students should refer to the next two chapters whenever they have a question about writing paragraphs or essays. Guidelines for writing explanations and for writing about people, places, objects, and events are also provided here.

Searching & Researching

■ The Research Paper
■ Writing with a Computer
■ Writing Summaries
■ Using the Library

The opening chapter covers everything a writer needs to know about the research process—from the steps in developing a research paper to documenting various sources of information. **Both MLA and APA documentation styles are covered in the handbook.** (The APA style is found in "The Appendix.") Guidelines for doing computer-assisted writing; writing abstracts, paraphrases, and précis; and finding information in the library are covered in the other chapters.

Special Forms of Writing

■ Writing the Poem
■ Writing the Short Story
■ Writing the News Story
■ Writing about Literature
■ Understanding Literature
■ Writing Letters, Memos, Résumés

The first two chapters give students a unique insider's look at writing poems and short stories. "Writing the News Story" helps students develop straight news stories, feature stories, and editorials. "Writing about Literature" discusses both writing the book review and keeping a reading log. "Understanding Literature" lists literary terms common to any study of literature. Guidelines for all types of business writing complete this section.

Reading & Learning

- Improving Reading and Vocabulary
- Classroom Skills
- Writing to Learn
- Test-Taking Skills
- College-Prep Skills

This section helps students take charge of their own learning. The opening chapter provides insights into academic reading and vocabulary building. "Classroom Skills" and "Writing to Learn" help students become actively involved in their course work. A special feature in "Classroom Skills" is the discussion of cooperative group skills. "Test-Taking Skills" addresses all types of academic tests, including the essay test; "College-Prep Skills" helps secondary students prepare for college.

Speaking & Thinking

- Speech Skills
- The Thinking Process
- Thinking Creatively
- Thinking Clearly
- Thinking Logically

"Speech Skills" provides students with everything they need to know about the speech-making process. The four chapters which follow present an excellent overview of the thinking process. The chapters on "Thinking Creatively" and "Thinking Logically" will be especially helpful to student writers.

Final Re-marks: A Proofreader's Guide

- Marking Punctuation
- Checking Mechanics
- Using the Right Word
- Understanding Grammar
- Treating the Sexes Fairly

Any questions students might have when they are proofreading papers are answered in this handy, user-friendly guide. This guide is completely indexed and color coded for quick reference.

Appendix

- Tables, Maps, and Useful Lists
- APA Research Paper Style

"The Appendix" helps make *Writers INC* work across the curriculum. It includes, among other things, symbols, conversion charts and tables, full-color maps, and historical documents. (It also includes guidelines to the APA research paper style.)

How is all of this information arranged in the handbook?

Writers INC can serve as the perfect handbook for students and teachers in high school (and beyond), one which will help students improve their ability **to write** (prewriting through proofreading), **to think** (creatively, logically, and clearly), and **to learn** (in the classroom, in small groups, independently). This quick tour will highlight the major points of interest and design in the handbook.

- ■ **Creative, User-Friendly Format**
- ■ **Stimulating Illustrations**
- ■ **Student-Written Samples**
- ■ **Clear, Step-by-Step Explanations**
- ■ **Numerous Guidelines, Summaries, and Checklists**
- ■ **Easy-to-Use Index**
- ■ **Useful Proofreader's Guide**
- ■ **Curriculum-Wide References**

"Writing is mind traveling, destination unknown."

Read the bold statement above, read it again, repeat it after every meal, have it tattooed on your arm. And by all means remember it as you work on your writing assignments. Let this statement be a constant reminder that when you write, you are often engaged in uncharted thinking, mind traveling, so to speak, in which you stumble upon old memories, face realities of the present, and confront hidden thoughts and feelings about what is yet to be. You won't necessarily know where your writing will take you, at least not at the beginning. Your destination will only become clear as you travel further and further into your writing and make new discoveries and uncover new ideas.

This is why writing may frighten some of you. You feel you must know "where" you are going before you start your journey. That is, you feel your route must be mapped out before you travel, so that you don't wander off course and end up lost. But writing rarely works that way. Instead, most writing works best when it is the product of a detour, an unexpected thought burst, an ordinary idea gone haywire.

And this is how writing works best for all writers—even professionals. Do you think writers like Robert Frost or James Baldwin knew what they were going to say before they started a poem or novel? No. They began each work with a general idea in mind and started writing (searching, experimenting, playing) to see what would develop. They realized that somewhere in their journey a "destination" would appear, perhaps faintly at first, and that eventually a clearer focus and form would emerge. In other words, they fully realized that they must do some mind traveling if they hoped to discover something worth writing about.

"For me the initial delight is in the surprise of remembering something I didn't know I knew. . . . I have never started a poem yet whose end I knew. Writing a poem is a discovery."

– Robert Frost

The Writing Process 5

Students will appreciate the clever illustrations and personal tone used throughout *Writers INC*.

Students will also appreciate the step-by-step instructions and helpful guidelines and checklists.

— Guidelines for Selecting a Subject —

031   The following activities will help you find a worthwhile starting point for your writing. Read through the entire list before you choose an activity to begin your subject search. *Note:* The more activities you attempt, the more potential writing subjects you will discover.

1. **Journal Writing** Write on a regular basis in a journal. Explore your personal feelings, develop your thoughts, and record the happenings of each day. Underline ideas in your personal writing that you would like to explore in writing assignments. (See 001 for a detailed explanation of personal writing.)

2. **Free Writing** Write nonstop for ten minutes to discover possible writing ideas. Begin writing with a particular focus in mind; otherwise, pick up on something that has recently attracted your attention. (See 035 for a detailed explanation of free writing.)

3. **Clustering** Begin a cluster with a *nucleus word*. Select a word that is related to your writing topic or assignment. For example, suppose you were to write an essay on responsibility and what it means to you. *Responsibility* or *duty* would be an obvious nucleus word. Record words which come to mind when you think of this word. Don't pick and choose; record every word. Circle each word as you write it, and draw a line connecting it to the closest related word. (See the cluster example below.)

"Clustering is that magic key. In fact, it is the master key to natural writing. It is the crucial first step . . . to touch the mental life of daydream, random thought, remembered image . . . "
—Gabriele Rico

    After three or four minutes of clustering, you will probably be ready to write. Scan your cluster for a word or idea that will get you going and write nonstop for about eight minutes. A writing subject should begin to develop from your clustering and writing.

4. **Listing** Freely listing ideas as they come to mind is another effective technique for searching for a writing subject. Begin with an idea or key word related to your assignment and simply start listing words.
Note: **Brainstorming**—the gathering and listing of ideas in groups—can also be an effective and enjoyable way to search for writing ideas.

24   *The Writing Process*

Opening quotations help set the tone for the advice and guidelines that follow.

"With every choice you make, you create a style. Your style, like your set of fingerprints, is yours, and only yours."

Think about your hair. This morning when you first yawned into the mirror, you had to choose: Shall I wash my hair? Shall I comb it? Shall I blow it dry? Shall I use mousse, gel, spritz, or some other glop? Shall I try something new? Shall I braid it, cornrow it, rubber band it, slick it, toss it, or just leave it? Do I want my football number shaved in back or shall I get a mohawk? Whatever you do—or don't do—that is *your style.*

Your writing style, similarly, comes from a series of choices that makes your writing yours. It is your words, your sentences, and your paragraphs and nobody else's. Fortunately, as a writer, you don't have to change your *'do* every month or two to be in fashion. Your writing will always be in style if it exhibits the traits of effective writing which follow.

Traits of an Effective Style

050   Evaluate your writing style in a particular piece of writing using the following guidelines:

Originality   To be original, writing must spring from your own fresh look at the subject matter, a new encounter with reality. Say what you think and feel, not what you assume others expect you to say.

Awareness   Aware writing shows sensitivity to the current events at the time of its composition. Notice what is going on around you—in your school, your neighborhood, your community, and the world in general. Then, if it applies, relate this information to your topic.

Vitality   Vital writing is lively. It crackles with energy and has a sense of purpose. Instead of a lazy, "just-get-it-done" feeling, it shows signs of conviction and life: growth, warmth, movement, interaction with the environment. The words and thoughts leap out at you instead of lying dead on the page. The use of vivid verbs, fresh images, and twisted phrases will lend vitality to your writing.

Variety   Variety in writing is the interplay of differences everywhere—among vowels and consonants, words and phrases, sound and meaning. Variety comes from connec-

Writing with Style   **33**

Students are often given creative as well as traditional approaches to writing and learning.

"We live in a time that allows writers freedom to choose what they investigate, to follow their thoughts wherever they lead, and to use a variety of styles and strategies. Therefore, the essay thrives...."

— Donald Hall

Writing
ESSAYS

Choosing an Approach

A good deal of your academic writing is essay writing. Themes are essays as are book reports or book reviews. You take essay tests; you write procedure (how-to) papers; some of you write editorials. All of these are essays—writing in which you explain, argue, describe, or interpret your thinking on a particular topic. The way you develop an essay depends on the guidelines established by your instructor and your own good judgment about a particular writing idea. For some essays, a straightforward, traditional approach might be best; for others, a more creative approach might be more effective.

No matter what approach you take when you write an essay, keep in mind that it is a demanding form of writing. You must understand your writing idea, have confidence in your position, and then develop it so that your readers can clearly share in your thinking.

Two Case Studies:

105   **The Traditional Essay**

Sarah wrote a paper about one of America's most important resources: oil. The fact that the U.S. is so dependent on foreign oil is what particularly interested her. Her paper specifically addresses the effects that the 1973 oil crisis had on America. This is the topic proposed in her opening paragraph. She develops it by describing how the oil crisis disrupted American life during that year.

Her first developmental paragraph describes the initial effects of the crisis that summer; her second paragraph describes the effects later that fall; her third paragraph describes the effects at the end of the year. Sarah's closing paragraph ties all of the important points together and draws a final conclusion for her readers. Her paper is clear, logical, and to the point—a classic five-paragraph composition. (See 116.)

106   **The Creative Essay**

Rudy wrote a paper about a critical international issue: world hunger. The fact that there are so many starving people in the world today particularly disturbs him. His paper

Writing the Essay   **53**

---

136   *"Research paper — report — what's the difference?"*

Join one of Ms. Marmalade's more "notorious" students during a writing conference and learn what it means to write a research paper.

You Ain't Nothin' But a Hound Dog

Ms. Marmalade: Your first draft is interesting, Elvis, but it really isn't a *research paper.* I would call this a *report.*

Elvis: Research paper—report—what's the difference? I went to two different encyclopedias and a book about the history of rock, and I wrote down everything there was about the origins of rock and roll. I wrote the same paper—I mean the same kind of paper—in junior high.

Ms. Marmalade: That was fine for a report. But a research paper requires a more active brand of thinking.

Elvis: I was sure active. My head was splittin' by the time I was through.

Ms. Marmalade: By "active" I mean *intellectually* active. In a report, you collect, organize, and compile information. You depend on experts to ask the right questions and give the right answers. You're an observer. Thus your role is essentially passive.

Elvis: Well, I worked up a mighty big sweat for being passive.

Ms. Marmalade: I'm sure you did, Elvis. But in a research paper, you're no longer simply an observer. You choose a topic that is open for debate. Then you gather information from many different sources and develop your own position.

Elvis: But half the time, they don't even agree!

Ms. Marmalade: Exactly. That's why you must formulate your own position or thesis and develop it as no one has ever done before. You become an authority on your topic by borrowing, comparing, rejecting, or agreeing with your sources; and explaining your own thinking as you go. That can be quite satisfying, Elvis.

Elvis: I get your point. *Now* will you take a peek at my new song?

Ms. Marmalade: I would be delighted. Hm. Very good. However, "ain't" is not proper diction, and "ain't nothin'" is a double negative. "Hound dog" is redundant and a bit general as well. This is a charming little tune, Elvis, but as you see, it needs some editing. A correct title would be, "You Are Nothing But a Bassett Hound." Be more careful when you edit the final draft of your research paper.

Elvis: Ms. Marmalade? No offense, ma'am, but you're stepping on my blue suede shoes, if you know what I mean. "Blue suede . . . you can do anything, but . . ."— hot dawg! I just got me an idea for another song!

Research Update

137   For years, student researchers have been burdened with the form of their finished product. If you have ever written a research paper with endnotes or footnotes, a working or complete bibliography, title page, etc., you know how much time and effort it takes just to understand the form of a research paper. Form so consumed student writers that content often became a secondary issue. What was said, in essence, was less important than how it was presented.

Current research style has changed this. The most widely used styles developed by the Modern Language Association of America (MLA) and the American Psychological Association (APA) are simple and efficient. They allow student researchers to devote most of their time to the important issue—developing meaningful research. A writer no longer has to struggle, for example, with footnotes at the bottom of a page or variations in line spacing. Preparing the finished product has become the important final step in the research process rather than an all-consuming one.

70   *The Research Paper*

Whenever appropriate, students are provided with entertaining and informative scenarios, situations, or scripts to make a point.

Topic numbers will help students easily locate the terms, definitions, and guidelines used throughout the handbook.

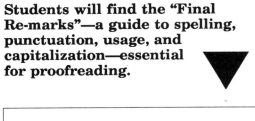

Students will find the "Final Re-marks"—a guide to spelling, punctuation, usage, and capitalization—essential for proofreading.

The following is the excerpt from the "Understanding Literature" page:

Understanding LITERATURE

"Every short story, at least for me, is a little act of discovery."
—Mary McCarthy

Literary Terms

275 An **abstract** word or phrase refers to an idea rather than a concrete object or thing. *Liberty, prejudice, love,* and *freedom* are examples of abstract words.

276 **Action** is what happens in a story: the events or conflicts. If the action is well organized, it will develop into a pattern or plot.

277 **Allegory** is a story in which people, things, and actions represent an idea or generalization about life; allegories often have a strong moral or lesson.

278 An **allusion** is a reference in literature to a familiar person, place, thing, or event.

279 An **analogy** is a comparison of two or more similar objects so as to suggest that if they are alike in certain respects, they will probably be alike in other ways as well.

280 **Anecdote** is a short summary of a funny or humorous event. Abe Lincoln was famous for his anecdotes, especially this one:

Two fellows, after a hot dispute over how long a man's legs should be in proportion to his body, stormed into Lincoln's office one day and confronted him with their problem. Lincoln listened intently to the arguments given by each of the men and after some reflection rendered his verdict: "This question has been a source of controversy for untold ages," he said, slowly and deliberately, "and it is about time it should be definitely decided. It has led to bloodshed in the past, and there is no reason to suppose it will not lead to the same in the future.
"After much thought and consideration, not to mention mental worry and anxiety, it is my opinion, all side issues being swept aside, that a man's lower limbs, in order to preserve harmony of proportion, should be at least long enough to reach from his body to the ground."

281 **Antagonist** is the person or thing working against the protagonist or hero of the work. When this is a person, he is usually called the *villain.*

152   *Understanding Literature*

The following is the excerpt from the "Marking Punctuation" page:

Marking PUNCTUATION

Period

600 A **period** is used to end a sentence which makes a statement, or which gives a command that is not used as an exclamation.

"That guy is coming over here."
"Don't forget to smile when you talk."
"Hello, Big Boy."
"Hi."

It is not necessary to place a period after a statement which has parentheses around it and is part of another sentence.

Euny gave Jim an earwich (an earwich is one piece of buttered bread slapped on each ear) and ran for her life.

601 An **ellipsis** (three periods) is used to show that one or more words have been omitted in a quotation. (Leave one space before and after each period when typing.)

"Give me your tired . . . yearning to breathe free."

If an omission occurs at the end of a sentence, the ellipsis is placed after the period which marks the conclusion of the sentence.

"Ernest Hemingway was fond of fishing. . . . His understanding of that sport is demonstrated in many of his writings."

Note: If the quoted material is a complete sentence (even if it was not in the original) use a period, then an ellipsis.

An ellipsis also may be used to indicate a pause.

"Well, Dad, I . . . ah . . . ran out of gas . . . had two flat tires . . . and ah . . . there was a terrible snowstorm on the other side of town."

602 A period should be placed after an initial.

Dena W. Kloosterman, Thelma J. Slenk, D. H. Lawrence

Marking Punctuation   257

The final section contains information students will find useful in all their classes, not just English class.

330   *Appendix*

A Section-by-Section tour of *Writers INC*

The Writing Process

SUMMARY: This section introduces students to writing as a process of exploration and discovery rather than an end product. The four steps discussed in the handbook address different aspects of the writing process. **Prewriting** helps students search for potential writing ideas, experiment with them, and eventually focus on one for writing. **Writing the First Draft** offers suggestions for developing an idea in an initial writing. **Revising** helps students rethink, rework, and refine their writing. **Editing** offers assistance when students are ready to fine-tune a piece of writing for publication. "Writing Guidelines" at the end of this section offers students clear and concise guidelines for everything from the writing process to shaping a potential writing idea.

SECTION SAMPLER:

The introduction emphasizes the exploratory nature of writing.

"Understanding the Process" puts writing in the proper perspective for student writers.

Special attention is given to the two most critical steps in the writing process—prewriting and revising.

"Guidelines for Selecting a Subject" (part of "Writing Guidelines") offers stimulating starting points for writing.

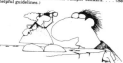

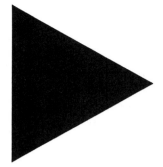

Popular Spots in "The Writing Process"

Writers will turn often to these popular spots in *Writers INC* for help and advice on using the writing process:

Minilesson: Using the Writing Process

Butcher, Baker, Candlestick Maker . . . . *Selecting a Topic*

Find an "Essentials of Life Checklist" near the end of the chapter on "The Writing Process" in *Writers INC*.

CHOOSE one item from each of the four columns.

MAKE UP four characters, each one associated with one of your four "essentials of life."

BEGIN to write a story which includes all four characters.

WRITE fast and freely for 5-8 minutes; then stop and jot down notes that will help you finish the story later.

*(See the **"INClings"** section in this guide for additional minilesson ideas.)*

Style & Form

SUMMARY: This section provides insights into writing style and two basic forms of writing: the paragraph and the essay. "Writing with Style" first addresses the traits of effective writing and then looks at the common stylistic "ailments" that can weaken writing. "Writing Paragraphs" discusses the basic elements of this writing form, plus a number of elements which pertain to writing in general. "Writing Essays" offers everything from the steps in the essay writing process to detailed guidelines for writing about people, places, objects, etc.

SECTION SAMPLER:

The engaging opening remarks about style speak directly to student writers.

■

"Improving Sentence Style" addresses everything a writer needs to know about sentence style—from common errors to clarity, from balance to appropriateness.

"With every choice you make, you create a style. Your style, like your set of fingerprints, is yours, and only yours."

Think about your hair. This morning when you first yawned into the mirror, you had to choose: Shall I wash my hair? Shall I comb it? Shall I blow it dry? Shall I use mousse, gel, spritz, or some other glop? Shall I try something new? Shall I braid it, cornrow it, rubber band it, slick it, toss it, or just leave it? Do I want my football number shaved in back or shall I get a mohawk? Whatever you do—or don't do—that is *your style.*

Your writing style, similarly, comes from a series of choices that makes your writing yours. It is your words, your sentences, and your paragraphs and nobody else's. Fortunately, as a writer, you don't have to change your *'do* every month or two to be in fashion. Your writing will always be in style if it exhibits the traits of effective writing which follow.

Traits of an Effective Style

050 Evaluate your writing style in a particular piece of writing using the following guidelines:

Originality To be original, writing must spring from your own fresh look at the subject matter, a new encounter with reality. Say what you think and feel, not what you assume others expect you to say.

Awareness Aware writing shows sensitivity to the current events at the time of its composition. Notice what is going on around you—in your school, your neighborhood, your community, and the world in general. Then, if it applies, relate this information to your topic.

Improving Sentence Style

"To err is human, but when the eraser wears out ahead of the pencil, you're overdoing it."
—J. Jenkins

Complete & Mature

With a few exceptions in special situations, you should use complete sentences when you write. By definition, a complete sentence expresses a complete thought. However, a sentence may actually contain several ideas, not just one. The trick is getting those ideas to work together to form mature, colorful sentences that are interesting to read. Among the most common errors made when attempting to write complete (and effective) sentences are **fragments, comma splices, run-ons,** and **rambling sentences.**

058 A **fragment** is a group of words used as a sentence. It is not a sentence, though, since it lacks a subject, a verb, or some other essential part which is needed to complete the thought. *Note:* Fragments are sometimes used in fiction, especially in dialogue.

Fragment:	Gradually, the delicate, lacy colors of spring. (This phrase lacks a verb.)
Sentence:	Gradually, the delicate, lacy colors of spring covered the hillside.
Fragment:	The minute she stepped into the barn. (This clause lacks a subject and a verb which are needed to complete the thought of what happened "The minute she stepped into the barn.")
Sentence:	The minute she stepped into the barn, cats darted in every direction.
Fragment:	She reached into her pocket. Searching from side to side for that last lump of sugar. (This is a sentence followed by a fragment. This error can be corrected by combining the fragment with the sentence.)
Sentence:	She reached into her pocket, searching from side to side for that last lump of sugar.

059 A **comma splice** is a mistake made when two independent clauses are *spliced* together with only a comma. (Also called a comma fault.)

Splice:	The concert crowd had been waiting in the hot sun for two hours, many of the people were beginning to show their impatience by chanting and clapping.
Corrected:	The concert crowd had been waiting in the hot sun for two hours. Many of the people were beginning to show their impatience by chanting and clapping. (Comma has been changed to a period.)
Corrected:	The concert crowd had been waiting in the hot sun for two hours, and many of the people were beginning to show their impatience by chanting and clapping. (Coordinating conjunction *and* has been added.)
	The concert crowd had been waiting in the hot sun for two hours; many of the people were beginning to show their impatience by chanting and clapping. (Comma has been changed to a semicolon. See 620.)

corrected by rearranging the ideas in a sentence.

ne of the players stands in front of the net and tries to keep e puck from going in, he is called the goalie.
ne of the players, called the goalie, stands in front of the net d tries to keep the puck from going in.

"We live in a time that allows writers freedom to choose what they investigate, to follow their thoughts wherever they lead, and to use a variety of styles and strategies. Therefore, the essay thrives...."
— Donald Hall

Writing ESSAYS

Choosing an Approach

A good deal of your academic writing is essay writing. Themes are essays as are book reports or book reviews. You take essay tests; you write procedure (how-to) papers; some of you write editorials. All of these are essays—writing in which you explain, argue, describe, or interpret your thinking on a particular topic. The way you develop an essay depends on the guidelines established by your instructor and your own good judgment about a particular writing idea. For some essays, a straightforward, traditional approach might be best; for others, a more creative approach might be more effective.

No matter what approach you take when you write an essay, keep in mind that it is a demanding form of writing. You must understand your writing idea, have confidence in your position, and then develop it so that your readers can clearly share in your thinking.

Two Case Studies:

105 The Traditional Essay

Sarah wrote a paper about one of America's most important resources: oil. The fact that the U.S. is so dependent on foreign oil is what particularly interested her. Her paper specifically addresses the effects that the 1973 oil crisis had on America. This is the topic proposed in her opening paragraph. She develops it by describing how the oil crisis disrupted American life during that year.

Her first developmental paragraph describes the initial effects of the crisis that summer; her second paragraph describes the effects later that fall; her third paragraph describes the effects at the end of the year. Sarah's closing paragraph ties all of her important points together and draws a final conclusion for her readers. Her paper is clear, logical, and to the point—a classic five-paragraph composition. (See 116.)

106 The Creative Essay

Rudy wrote a paper about a critical international issue: world hunger. The fact that there are so many starving people in the world today particularly disturbs him. His paper

Writing to Persuade

125 When you write to persuade, you write to prove a point, to change someone's opinion, to clarify an issue. Persuading someone to change his or her mind or take a stand is not always easy. It requires careful thinking and planning, strong evidence or support, and a thorough understanding of the topic.

More than any other type of writing, persuasive writing requires that you select a subject which truly interests you, one which you have strong feelings about. Your subject *(issue)* should be current and controversial.

1. Reflect Begin collecting material by free writing, clustering, or listing your personal feelings about the issue and the reasons you feel the way you do. This may be the most important stage in the persuasive writing process; you simply cannot be convincing unless you have "you" on your side.

2. Investigate Talk to other people about the issue. What are their feelings about the issue and why do they feel this way? What personal experiences have they had that make them feel this way? What would they suggest be done to solve or lessen the problem? Listen carefully, especially to those with whom you disagree. They will give you a preview of the response you can expect from your audience. Test your opinions and reasons on them. You must understand well what you are up against if you hope to write persuasively.

3. Read Read as much as you can about the issue. Understand fully the history of the issue and what events or circumstances led up to the way things are today. Gather facts, figures, evidence, examples, and quotations—on both sides of the issue. Read current periodicals so that you are both informed and up-to-date.

4. Think For writing to be persuasive, it must be founded in logic. (See "Thinking Logically.") Use a calm, reasoning tone throughout your writing. Rely on logic, not emotion. Be diplomatic. Give credit to the reasonable arguments on the other side of the issue; then point out clearly the weaknesses of each. Admit that this issue, as with most, is not a black and white issue. Then, convince your reader that your perspective is the most sensible, logical one.

5. Organize Persuasive writing should be well organized. Here are some suggestions:

a. Write out a clear statement of the purpose behind your persuasive writing. This statement (often called a *proposition*) should spell out what you propose to prove in your writing. State your proposition in positive terms. ("School officials should be prohibited from secretly searching student lockers," rather than "... officials should not be allowed to ....")

b. Place your topic *(proposition)* at the top of your paper. List your reasons underneath; under each reason, list the facts, figures, examples, or quotations which help support it.

c. Use specific examples to illustrate your main points. Build strong images: "Each day this country throws out enough garbage to completely cover the state of Rhode Island." Use statistics sparingly and, when you do, round them off: "Each day we throw out nearly 50 million tons of garbage."

d. Appeal to the needs of your reader. Let each of them know what's in it for him or her. Prove to them that they have something to gain by taking the same stand as you. Use stylistic devices (if needed) to draw attention to the important points you are trying to make.

e. Choose your words carefully. Remember that words convey feeling (*connotation*) as well as meaning (*denotation*). Select words which your reader will react to positively. (Define any words which your reader may not be familiar with.)

f. Consider ending your writing with one of your strongest examples or reasons. Your readers may well hold judgment until the very end, waiting for "the bottom line."

Writers are offered a choice of different writing strategies so they can develop essays in a way that works best for them.

■

Writers will refer to the guidelines for writing to persuade, explain, and describe time and time again.

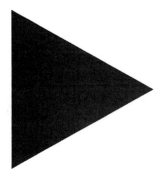

Popular Spots in "Style & Form"

Writers will turn often to these popular spots in *Writers INC* for ways to improve the style and form of their writing:

Minilesson: Style & Form

Fresh as a Daisy . . . . *More About Style*

In the section "Improving Sentence Style" (**058-082**), read the subsection titled "Concise & Natural."

PICK OUT something you've written lately—a story or an essay.

CIRCLE any example of deadwood, flowery language, triteness, euphemism, jargon, or cliche that you find.

REWRITE any sentence with a circle in it, using fresh language.

Searching & Researching

SUMMARY: The opening chapter covers everything a writer needs to know about the research process—from what it means to be a researcher to the steps in the research process, from documenting sources to computer-assisted writing. "Writing Summaries" provides insights into writing abstracts, paraphrases, and précis and samples of each. "Using the Library" helps researchers take full advantage of information contained in the library.

SECTION SAMPLER:

The research process is put into perspective in the opening pages of "Searching & Researching."

■

The steps in the research process are clearly and thoroughly described—from selecting an interesting subject to proofreading the final draft.

The extensive lists of sample parenthetical references and Works Cited entries follow MLA guidelines. (APA guidelines are included in a separate section.)

■

Students can follow the development of a fellow researcher's finished product in the fully annotated model.

Popular Spots in "Searching & Researching"

Writers will turn often to these popular spots in *Writers INC* to locate helpful information in the researching process:

Minilesson: Searching & Researching

Running Short · *Writing a Précis*

Read the traditional essay, "America—The Land of Plenty?" (**116**).
STUDY the "Guidelines for Writing a Précis" (**182**).
Without looking back at it, WRITE a précis of "America—The Land of Plenty?"
CHECK your précis against the original.

Special Forms of Writing

SUMMARY: The opening two chapters on poetry and short stories are much more than how-to pieces about writing short fiction. Each chapter gives student writers a real feel for these two special forms of writing. "Writing the News Story" provides insights into writing straight news stories, feature stories, and editorials. "Writing about Literature" discusses writing the book review and keeping a reading log. The section that follows—"Understanding Literature"—lists the literary terms common to any study of literature. Guidelines for all types of business writing complete this section.

SECTION SAMPLER:

In "The Poet in You," students see that poetry has always been a part of their lives.

"Anatomy of a Short Story Writer" provides valuable advice for all writers.

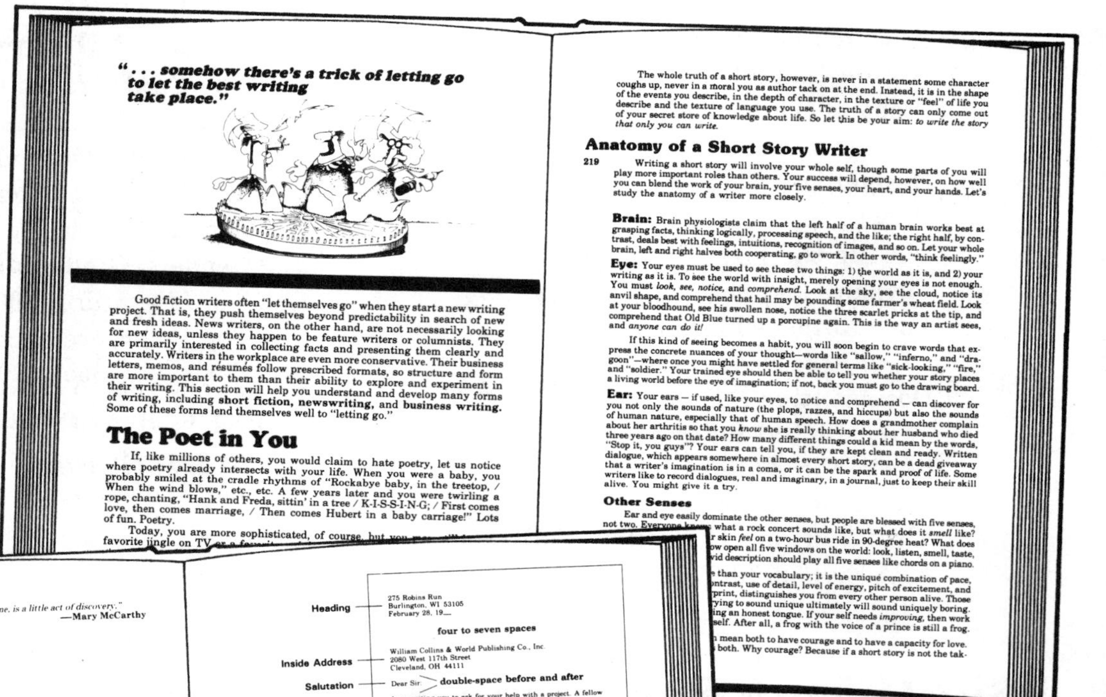

> "... somehow there's a trick of letting go to let the best writing take place."

Good fiction writers often "let themselves go" when they start a new writing project. That is, they push themselves beyond predictability in search of new and fresh ideas. News writers, on the other hand, are not necessarily looking for new ideas, unless they happen to be feature writers or columnists. They are primarily interested in collecting facts and presenting them clearly and accurately. Writers in the workplace are even more conservative. Their business letters, memos, and résumés follow prescribed formats, so structure and form are more important to them than their ability to explore and experiment in their writing. This section will help you understand and develop many forms of writing, including short fiction, newswriting, and business writing. Some of these forms lend themselves well to "letting go."

The Poet in You

If, like millions of others, you would claim to hate poetry, let us notice where poetry already intersects with your life. When you were a baby, you probably smiled at the cradle rhythms of "Rockabye baby, in the treetop, / When the wind blows," etc., etc. A few years later and you were twirling a rope, chanting, "Hank and Freda, sittin' in a tree / K-I-S-S-I-N-G; First comes love, then comes marriage, / Then comes Hubert in a baby carriage!" Lots of fun. Poetry.

Today, you are more sophisticated, of course, but you may still have a favorite jingle on TV or a favorite...

The whole truth of a short story, however, is never in a statement some character coughs up, never in a moral you as author tack on at the end. Instead, it is in the shape of the events you describe, in the depth of character, in the texture or "feel" of life you describe and the texture of language you use. The truth of a story can only come out of your secret store of knowledge about life. So let this be your aim: *to write the story that only you can write.*

Anatomy of a Short Story Writer

219   Writing a short story will involve your whole self, though some parts of you will play more important roles than others. Your success will depend, however, on how well you can blend the work of your brain, your five senses, your heart, and your hands. Let's study the anatomy of a writer more closely.

Brain: Brain physiologists claim that the left half of a human brain works best at grasping facts, thinking logically, processing speech, and the like; the right half, by contrast, deals best with feelings, intuitions, recognition of images, and so on. Let your whole brain, left and right halves both cooperating, go to work. In other words, "think feelingly."

Eye: Your eyes must be used to see these two things: 1) the world as it is, and 2) your writing as it is. To see the world with insight, merely opening your eyes is not enough. You must *look, see, notice,* and *comprehend.* Look at the sky, see the cloud, notice its anvil shape, and comprehend that hail may be pounding some farmer's wheat field. Look at your bloodhound, see his swollen nose, notice the three scarlet pricks at the tip, and comprehend that Old Blue turned up a porcupine again. This is the way an artist sees, *and anyone can do it!*

If this kind of seeing becomes a habit, you will soon begin to crave words that express the concrete nuances of your thought—words like "sallow," "inferno," and "dragoon"—where once you might have settled for general terms like "sick-looking," "fire," and "soldier." Your trained eye should then be able to tell you whether your story places a living world before the eye of imagination; if not, back you must go to the drawing board.

Ear: Your ears—if used, like your eyes, to notice and comprehend—can discover for you not only the sounds of nature (the plops, razzes, and hiccups) but also the sounds of human nature, especially that of human speech. How does a grandmother complain about her arthritis so that you *know* she is really thinking about her husband who died three years ago on that date? How many different things could a kid mean by the words, "Stop it, you guys"? Your ears can tell you, if they are kept clean and ready. Written dialogue, which appears somewhere in almost every short story, can be a dead giveaway that a writer's imagination is in a coma, or it can be the spark and proof of life. Some writers like to record dialogues, real and imaginary, in a journal, just to keep their skill alive. You might give it a try.

Other Senses

Ear and eye easily dominate the other senses, but people are blessed with five senses, not two. Everyone knows what a rock concert sounds like, but what does it *smell* like? How does your skin *feel* on a two-hour bus ride in 90-degree heat? What does your tongue know? Throw open all five windows on the world: look, listen, smell, taste, touch. Your vivid description should play all five senses like chords on a piano.

...than your vocabulary; it is the unique combination of pace, ...trast, use of detail, level of energy, pitch of excitement, and ...print, distinguishes you from every other person alive. Those ...rying to sound unique ultimately will sound uniquely boring. ...ng an honest tongue. If your self needs *improving,* then work ...self. After all, a frog with the voice of a prince is still a frog.

...mean both to have courage and to have a capacity for love. ...both. Why courage? Because if a short story is not the tak...

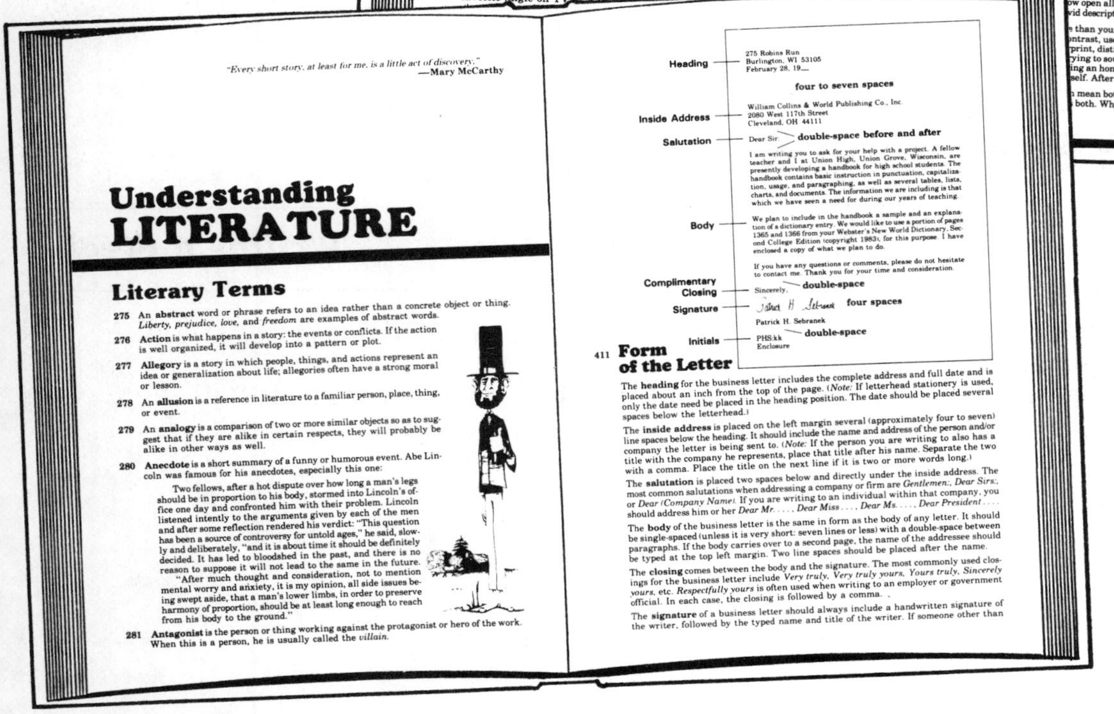

Literary terms are listed alphabetically and indexed for easy reference.

Sample annotated business letters provide an easy and quick reference for writers.

> "Every short story, at least for me, is a little act of discovery."
> —Mary McCarthy

Understanding LITERATURE

Literary Terms

275   An **abstract** word or phrase refers to an idea rather than a concrete object or thing. *Liberty, prejudice, love,* and *freedom* are examples of abstract words.

276   **Action** is what happens in a story: the events or conflicts. If the action is well organized, it will develop into a pattern or plot.

277   **Allegory** is a story in which people, things, and actions represent an idea or generalization about life; allegories often have a strong moral or lesson.

278   An **allusion** is a reference in literature to a familiar person, place, thing, or event.

279   An **analogy** is a comparison of two or more similar objects so as to suggest that if they are alike in certain respects, they will probably be alike in other ways as well.

280   **Anecdote** is a short summary of a funny or humorous event. Abe Lincoln was famous for his anecdotes, especially this one:

Two fellows, after a hot dispute over how long a man's legs should be in proportion to his body, stormed into Lincoln's office one day and confronted him with their problem. Lincoln listened intently to the arguments given by each of the men and after some reflection rendered his verdict: "This question has been a source of controversy for untold ages," he said, slowly and deliberately, "and it is about time it should be definitely decided. It has led to bloodshed in the past, and there is no reason to suppose it will not lead to the same in the future.

"After much thought and consideration, not to mention mental worry and anxiety, it is my opinion, all side issues being swept aside, that a man's lower limbs, in order to preserve harmony of proportion, should be at least long enough to reach from his body to the ground."

281   **Antagonist** is the person or thing working against the protagonist or hero of the work. When this is a person, he is usually called the **villain.**

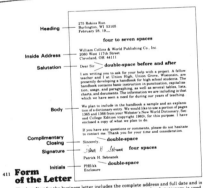

Heading	275 Robins Run Burlington, WI 53105 February 28, 19____
	← four to seven spaces
Inside Address	William Collins & World Publishing Co., Inc. 2080 West 117th Street Cleveland, OH 44111
Salutation	Dear Sir: ← double-space before and after
Body	I am writing you to ask for your help with a project. A fellow teacher and I at Union High, Union Grove, Wisconsin, are presently developing a handbook for high school students. The handbook contains basic instruction in punctuation, capitalization, usage, and paragraphing, as well as several tables, lists, charts, and documents. The information we are including is that which we have seen a need for during our years of teaching. We plan to include in the handbook a sample and an explanation of a dictionary entry. We would like to use a portion of pages 1365 and 1366 from your Webster's New World Dictionary, Second College Edition (copyright 1983), for this purpose. I have enclosed a copy of what we plan to do. If you have any questions or comments, please do not hesitate to contact me. Thank you for your time and consideration.
Complimentary Closing	Sincerely, ← double-space
Signature	*Robert H. Sebranek* ← four spaces Patrick H. Sebranek
Initials	PHS:kk ← double-space Enclosure

411 Form of the Letter

The **heading** for the business letter includes the complete address and full date and is placed about an inch from the top of the page. (*Note:* If letterhead stationery is used, only the date need be placed in the heading position. The date should be placed several spaces below the letterhead.)

The **inside address** is placed on the left margin several (approximately four to seven) line spaces below the heading. It should include the name and address of the person and/or company the letter is being sent to. (*Note:* If the person you are writing to also has a title with the company he represents, place that title after his name. Separate the two with a comma. Place the title on the next line if it is two or more words long.)

The **salutation** is placed two spaces below and directly under the inside address. The most common salutations when addressing a company or firm are *Gentlemen:, Dear Sirs:,* or *Dear (Company Name):* If you are writing to an individual within that company, you should address him or her *Dear Mr. ..., Dear Miss ..., Dear Ms. ..., Dear President...*

The **body** of the business letter is the same in form as the body of any letter. It should be single-spaced (unless it is very short: seven lines or less) with a double-space between paragraphs. If the body carries over to a second page, the name of the addressee should be typed at the top left margin. Two line spaces should be placed after the name.

The **closing** comes between the body and the signature. The most commonly used closings for the business letter include *Very truly, Very truly yours, Yours truly, Sincerely yours,* etc. *Respectfully yours* is often used when writing to an employer or government official. In each case, the closing is followed by a comma.

The **signature** of a business letter should always include a handwritten signature of the writer, followed by the typed name and title of the writer. If someone other than

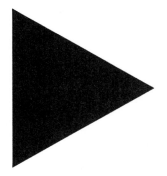

Popular Spots in "Special Forms of Writing"

Writers will turn often to these popular spots in *Writers INC* for help with the special forms of writing:

Minilesson: Special Forms of Writing

> **Poems from Paragraphs** . . . . *Choosing a Subject for a Poem*

Read the section on "Choosing a Subject [for a Poem]" (**213**). Focus on the first suggestion concerning "found poetry."

SEARCH through *Writers INC* for a passage of prose that has a poetic "ring" to it.
ORGANIZE the passage into poetic lines without changing the words.
PUT an interesting title on it.
PRESENT your work to someone as a "found poem."

Reading & Learning

SUMMARY: This section helps students take charge of their own learning. "Reading to Learn" provides insights into academic reading and vocabulary building. "Classroom Skills" and "Writing to Learn" help students become actively involved in their course work. A special feature in "Classroom Skills" is the discussion of cooperative group skills. "Taking Tests" addresses all types of academic tests—from essay tests to multiple choice tests, from true/false tests to matching tests. "College-Prep Skills" helps secondary students prepare for college.

SECTION SAMPLER:

A user-friendly tone is established with the opening quotation and illustration.

The dictionary of prefixes, suffixes, and roots is one of the many helpful items in "Improving Reading & Vocabulary."

Students can become actively involved in their course work by following the "Guidelines to Keeping a Learning Log."

"Writing-to-Learn Activities" provides students with a number of stimulating ways to learn through writing.

Popular Spots in "Reading & Learning"

Writers will turn often to these popular spots in *Writers INC* for ways to improve their reading and learning skills:

Minilesson: Using Reading & Learning

> **Strange Sentences** . . . . *Remembering What You Read*

Look at the full-color map of Africa in the appendix to *Writers INC*.
TRY to memorize the names of the nine largest countries in northern Africa. Having trouble?
  TURN to the section called "Strange Sentences," topic **437** under "Remembering What You Have Read."
  FOLLOW the instructions for using a "strange sentence" to memorize the names of the nine countries.
  WRITE DOWN your sentence. Did it work?

Speaking & Thinking

SUMMARY: "Speech Skills" provides students with everything they need to know about the speech-making process—from selecting a topic to writing the speech, from a close look at style and tone to evaluating a speech. The four chapters which follow present an excellent overview of the thinking process. The chapters on "Thinking Creatively" and "Thinking Logically" will be especially helpful to student writers.

SECTION SAMPLER:

The questions in "Starting Your Speech" will help student speech writers set out in the right direction.

■

"Developing a Formal Argument" provides students with the foundation for organizing and presenting their thoughts logically and persuasively.

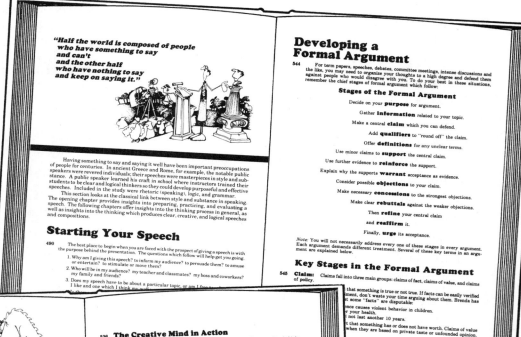

"Half the world is composed of people who have something to say and can't and the other half who have nothing to say and keep on saying it."

Having something to say and saying it well have been important preoccupations of people for centuries. In ancient Greece and Rome, for example, the notable public speakers were revered individuals; their speeches were masterpieces in style and substance. A public speaker learned his craft in school where instructors trained their students to be clear and logical thinkers so they could develop purposeful and effective speeches. Included in the study were rhetoric (speaking), logic, and grammar.

This section looks at the classical link between style and substance in speaking. The opening chapter provides insights into preparing, practicing, and evaluating a speech. The following chapters offer insights into the thinking process in general, as well as insights into the thinking which produces clear, creative, and logical speeches and compositions.

Starting Your Speech

490   The best place to begin when you are faced with the prospect of giving a speech is with the purpose behind the presentation. The questions which follow will help get you going.

1. Why am I giving this speech? to inform my audience? to persuade them? to amuse or entertain? to stimulate or move them?
2. Who will be in my audience? my teacher and classmates? my boss and coworkers? my family and friends?
3. Does my speech have to be about a particular topic, or am I free to...

Developing a Formal Argument

544   For term papers, speeches, debates, committee meetings, intense discussions and the like, you may need to organize your thoughts to a high degree and defend them against people who would disagree with you. To do your best in these situations, remember the chief stages of formal argument which follow:

Stages of the Formal Argument

Decide on your **purpose** for argument.

Gather **information** related to your topic.

Make a central **claim** which you can defend.

Add **qualifiers** to "round off" the claim.

Offer **definitions** for any unclear terms.

Use minor claims to **support** the central claim.

Use further evidence to **reinforce** the support.

Explain why the supports **warrant** acceptance as evidence.

Consider possible **objections** to your claim.

Make necessary **concessions** to the strongest objections.

Make clear **rebuttals** against the weaker objections.

Then **refine** your central claim

and **reaffirm** it.

Finally, **urge** its acceptance.

Note: You will not necessarily address every one of these stages in every argument. Each argument demands different treatment. Several of these key terms in an argument are explained below.

Key Stages in the Formal Argument

545   **Claim:**   Claims fall into three main groups: claims of fact, claims of value, and claims of policy.

...that something is true or not true. If facts can be easily verified ...ment, don't waste your time arguing about them. Brenda has ...t some "facts" are disputable.

...nce causes violent behavior in children.

...r your health.

...not last another 10 years.

...t that something has or does not have worth. Claims of value ...when they are based on private taste or unfounded opinion.

The Thinking PROCESS

Opening Thoughts

You don't have to *be* a brain to *use* your brain. In fact, as you read this page, you are already using the thinking skills a nuclear physicist, a fine artist, or a philosopher would use. You observe, name, add, distinguish, compare, analyze parts, shape parts into new wholes, form general ideas, evaluate things, and solve problems. Moreover, you were using those skills already in first grade, without even "thinking."

Apart from age and life experience, what is the difference between a first grader and a thinker like you? You have become more skilled over the years. You did it by

- using your brain more often,
- using more of your brain's potential,
- enlarging your aims,
- more consciously controlling the thinking process, and
- learning helpful techniques.

525   Before you go on, remember one thing. Only a small portion of a person's thinking takes place on the conscious level. Most of it goes on in the dark caverns of the subconscious mind. No logical rules or creative techniques can ever capture the whole process. Thoughts have to fight their way upstream like salmon. They swarm toward their destination like bees. They churn like a potful of boiling soup. Formal guidelines may help you start, stop, or steer your thoughts, but when they begin to stifle subconscious thoughts, they have lost their usefulness. Don't put your genius behind bars. Stay flexible. Keep it fun.

The section which follows will help you better understand and appreciate the thinking process. First, you'll take stock of your reasons for thinking; then you'll meet someone with a "thinking attitude"; and, finally, you'll learn about your thinking organ—the brain.

536   **The Creative Mind in Action**

Without creativity you might look at an ordinary object like a pencil and think, "There's a pencil. Something to write with. It looks brand new. It's probably worth less than a dime."

But if you look at the same pencil with a creative mind—not just look at it but notice it and feel it as it is—it can set all sorts of mental imagery in motion. Here's proof:

The No. 2 Pencil Meets a Creative Mind

- First, notice the parts: lead point, hexagonal wooden barrel painted yellow, words "Dixon Ticonderoga 1388—2 Soft" stamped along one side in green ink on gold, triple-striped green and yellow metal collar holding a powdery pink eraser, not yet rubbed raw.
- Imagine the manufacturing process—the wood gluers, the planes, the slicers, the paint vats, the dryers, the stamps, and so on.
- Think of the tree the wood was once a part of. Where did it grow? Where on the tree was this pencil's wood located? Where are the other parts of the tree now?
- Imagine the paint. Now imagine being covered all over with yellow paint and stamped with green and gold letters.
- See the pencil as a bridge stretching between two places. What are they?
- Imagine the pencil as a pillar. What is it holding up?
- Who will hold this pencil before it is worn to a nub? What will be the most important thing ever written with it? What will be the funniest thing?
- How strong is it? How much weight would be needed to break it? The weight of a safe? Of a hamster? A six-year-old boy? A rainbow trout?
- Now it is being used as a pointer. Who is pointing it and what are they pointing at? Why?
- Imagine an occasion when this pencil might be given as a gift. What is the occasion?
- If the pencil could think, what would it be thinking as it is locked away in a drawer? How about as it is being used to write a letter?
- How would you feel if you were turned upside down and your head, ground to a point, were scraped in loops and squiggles across a piece of paper?
- Imagine a world in which the pencil is a sacred object. What would that world be like?
- Look at the pencil—what does it resemble?
- Listen to the sounds it makes—what do they remind you of?
- Smell it—what does the smell remind you of?
- Bite it—what does it taste like?
- Roll the pencil around in your fingers—what does its texture bring to mind?

Get the idea? What other new ways of experiencing the pencil can you think of? Always be on the alert, thinking of new ways to look at old objects and ideas. *Remember:* When your brain has nothing to do, it has a way of freezing up. Use your brain, your creativity. See Velcro, not sandburs.

Students learn what it means to have a thinking attitude in this opening chapter on the thinking process.

■

"The Creative Mind in Action" makes the idea of creativity come alive for students.

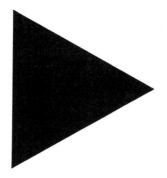

Popular Spots in "Speaking & Thinking"

Writers will turn often to these popular spots in *Writers INC* for help with speaking and thinking activities:

Minilesson: Using Speaking & Thinking

> ### A Room of One's Own . . . . . *The Creative Process: Sensory Perceptions*

Find "An Overview of the Creative Process" in *Writers INC* (**534**). Focus on the comments about "sensory perceptions."

CLOSE your eyes and recall a room where you have spent much time in the past. From your memory, draw one exact memory of a *sight*, one memory of a *sound*, one of a *smell*, one of a *taste*, and one of a *touch*.

OPEN your eyes and list these memories on paper, using words as exactly as you can.

REPEAT this process, with eyes open, for the room where you are now sitting.

CLOSE your eyes and imagine a room somewhere in your future; repeat the process of listing five sensory perceptions.

Your Final Re-marks: A Proofreader's Guide

SUMMARY: Any questions that students might have when they are proofreading their papers are answered in this guide. Many useful charts and lists appear throughout—including the list of commonly misspelled words (714) and the common irregular verbs and their principal parts (874). The guide is completely indexed and color coded for quick reference.

SECTION SAMPLER:

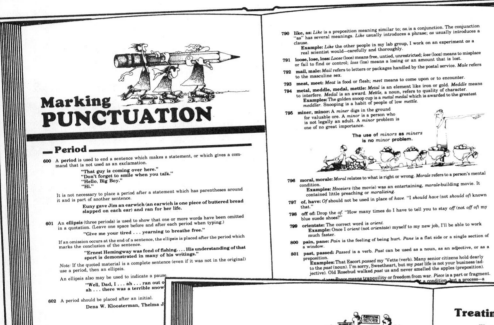

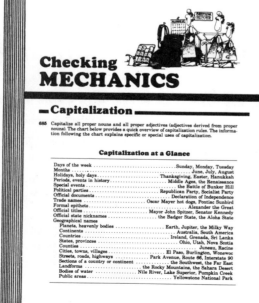

The rules for each punctuation mark are clearly explained and followed by helpful (and often entertaining) sample sentences.

■

The differences between the most commonly mixed pairs are clearly described in "Using the Right Word."

When is *father* or *mother* capitalized? The answer to that and any other questions of mechanics is found in this chapter.

■

"Treating the Sexes Fairly" addresses the issue of sexism in language.

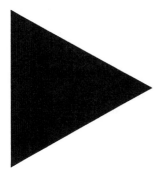

Popular Spots in "Final Re-marks"

Writers will turn often to these popular spots in *Writers INC* for help with their proofreading:

Marking Punctuation (600-681)

Checking Mechanics (685-714)

Using the Right Word (715-837)

Understanding Grammar (840-945)

Minilesson: Your Final Re-marks

My Uncle, the Jockey .... *Using Commas*

Study the rules for using commas to set off explanatory phrases (**607**).
    CHOOSE one of your parents or relatives.
    WRITE one sentence about who the person is.
    WRITE a second sentence about what the person does.
    COMBINE the two sentences, reducing the first sentence to an appositive phrase and
        using commas correctly.

The Appendix

SUMMARY: The appendix helps make *Writers INC* work across the curriculum. It includes, among other things, symbols, multiplication and division tables, conversion charts, and decimal equivalents of fractions for math and science students. For history and social studies students, it includes maps and important documents. And for everyone's general knowledge, it includes items like traffic and guide signs, hand signs, and computer terms.

SECTION SAMPLER:

There is something for everyone in the appendix, as the table of contents attests.

■

What other writing and learning handbook lists the U.S. presidents and the order of presidential succession?

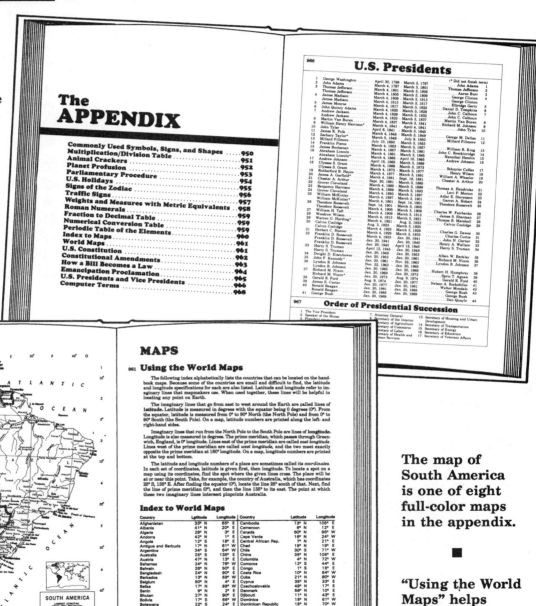

The map of South America is one of eight full-color maps in the appendix.

■

"Using the World Maps" helps students locate a country on a map using its coordinates.

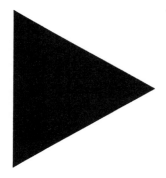

Popular Spots in "The Appendix"

Writers will turn often to these popular spots in *Writers INC* for help across the curriculum:

Science
Animal Crackers (952)
Planet Profusion (953)
Periodic Table of the Elements (960)

Math
Multiplication/Division Table (951)
Weights and Measures with Metric
    Equivalents (958)
Fraction to Decimal Table (959)
Numerical Conversion Table (959)
Computer Terms (968)

Social Studies
U.S. Constitution (962)
Constitutional Amendments (963)
How a Bill Becomes a Law (964)
Emancipation Proclamation (965)
U.S. Presidents and Vice Presidents (966)

Geography
Index to Maps (961)
World Maps (961)

General Knowledge
Commonly Used Symbols, Signs, and
    Shapes (950)
Parliamentary Procedure (954)
U.S. Holidays (955)
Signs of the Zodiac (956)
Traffic Signs (957)
Roman Numerals (959)

Minilesson: Using the Appendix

We the People .... *Writing the Paraphrase*

Read the instructions for writing "The Paraphrase" in *Writers INC* (**181**).
    PRACTICE your paraphrasing skills by turning to the "Constitution of the United States"
    (**962-963**);
    READ and PARAPHRASE the "Preamble" (**962**) and the "First Amendment" (**963**).

Using *Writers INC* in the Classroom

Where does *Writers INC* fit in?

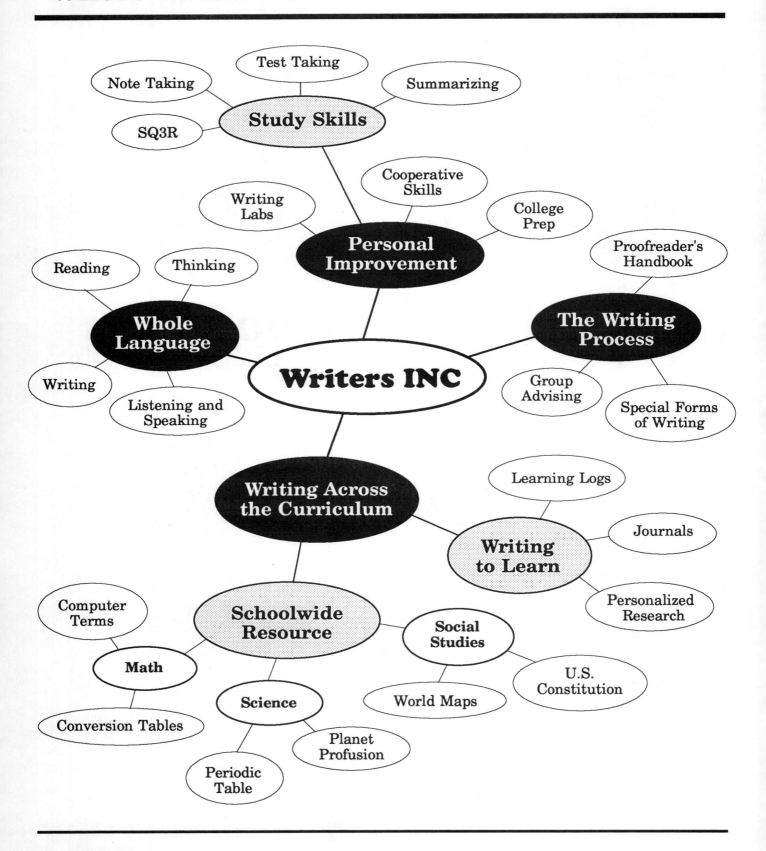

How can *Writers INC* be used in the language classroom?

Writers INC contains a great variety of information which allows it to be used in all language classes, from basic writing to advanced placement and everything in between. It was first developed for use by a group of teachers and students in Wisconsin who felt a need for a handbook to help them with the day-to-day business of reading, writing, speaking, and listening in their language classes. (Also see the *English Journal* article on pp. 30-31.)

Writers INC is suited for use in all English classes . . .

■ **Basic Communication/ Composition**
Keeping a Journal
The Writing Process
Academic Writing: The Paragraph and Essay
Improving Sentence Style
Writing Letters, Memos, and Résumés
Using the Library
Using a Dictionary and Thesaurus
Writing Summaries
Writing the Essay Test
Editing and Proofreading Guide: Usage, Punctuation, Mechanics, Grammar

■ **Literature**
Writing about Literature
Keeping a Reading Log
Understanding Literature/Literary Terms
Recommended Reading Lists
Using Context Clues

■ **Creative Writing**
Personal Writing
Writing the Poem
Writing the Short Story
Writing the Creative Essay
Writing with Style
Thinking Creatively

■ **Advanced Courses**
The Research Paper (MLA & APA)
College-Prep Skills
The Traditional Essay
The Book Review
Point of View/Diction
Writing Metaphorically
Common Ailments of Style
Writing an Abstract and Précis
Thinking Logically

■ **Journalism**
The News Story
The Feature Story
The Editorial
Journalism Terms

■ **Reading & Vocabulary**
Reading to Learn
Techniques for Adjusting Purpose and Rate
Study-Reading: SQ3R
Using Context Clues
Vocabulary Improvement
A Dictionary of Prefixes, Suffixes, and Roots
The Mechanics of Reading
Keeping a Reading Journal
Writing about Literature

■ **Speaking**
Planning the Speech
Writing the Speech
A Closer Look at Style
Delivering the Speech
Evaluating the Speech

■ **Learning and Study Skills**
Listening to Learn
Note-taking Skills
Cooperative Group Skills
Writing to Learn
Taking Tests
The Thinking Process
Thinking Clearly
Writing with a Computer

Using *Writers INC* In and Out of Class

Reprinted in part from   Volume 80, Number 7
November 1991

ENGLISH JOURNAL

User-Friendly English Handbooks

What is the most readable and useful English handbook or dictionary of usage that you know? How do you use it in your teaching?

We begin with a timely reminder that if all such handbooks went out of print, we'd be prompted perhaps to draft our own. James W. Penha does just that with his students and describes their three-page product as "the most useful handbook I've yet discovered in my high-school teaching."

Though many of us can recite rules like walking handbooks, our students don't necessarily plug in as easily. Their best way to become independent editors of written language, therefore, will be through familiarity with useful handbooks.

***Writers INC* amassed more recommendations than any other handbook,** and we have included three reviews to document its usefulness. . . .   EDN

Writers INC, formerly ***Basic English Revisited: A Student Handbook.***   Sebranek, Meyer, Kemper. Write Source, 1989, 354 pp. Softcover List: $9.95; School Price: (1-24) $7.95, (25+) $7.50. Hardcover List: $11.95; School Price: (1-24) $9.95, (25+) $9.50. ISBN 0-939045-48-6. A junior-high/middle-school version, *Write Source 2000*, is also available, and a full line of support products is listed in the catalog.

Mary Lou Edwards
Frewsburg Central School, New York 14738

What's yellow and black and zaps you with a sting? The answer is *Writers INC*, a handbook that contains a treasure trove of information.

It's compact, easy to carry, and includes valuable information on writing and reading. The title reveals all that's between the two bright yellow covers. Students who go to college return and tell me that the book is better than the seventeen-dollar handbook they've had to buy.

James Upton
Burlington Community High School, Iowa 52601

Writers INC, the most readable and used handbook I have discovered, has become a reference staple for students and staff. As a handbook for students, *Writers INC* includes a concise and practical language hand-book, valuable background and ideas about writing processes, research processes and products, thinking processes, writing-to-learn suggestions, and a variety of maps, tables, summaries, and charts from the "Periodic Table of the Elements" to traffic signs. More efficiently than any other handbook, *Writers INC*, affectionately called "Old Yeller" by students, provides students with clear and practical rules, models, and suggestions for almost all writing/learning tasks. "Look it up in Old Yeller" is a common admonition in classes.

For the teacher, *Writers INC* provides easy and effective remediation, reinforcement, and enrichment to almost any language-arts text and provides excellent supplementary information in writing to learn, study skills, research, and the like for use in all courses. I have used *Writers INC* as the basic text in writing courses, and one of the bonuses of the book is that the publisher has developed an excellent teacher's guide titled *INC Sights* which provides information about whole language, writing to learn, evaluating writing, and over one hundred minilessons using *Writers INC* as text. The publisher has also created two other supplementary books, *Revising & Editing One* and *Revising & Editing Two*, to provide students with practice in revising, editing, and proofreading.

Nancy Marquardsen
Durant High School, Iowa 52747

What makes *Writers INC* so valuable?

1. *Cost.* One handbook (School Price: [1-24] $7.95, [25+] $7.50 softcover) can be used at any or all grade levels. Currently I use a classroom set of *Basic English Revisited* for juniors. The college-prep seniors purchase their own copies of *Writers INC*.

2. *Size.* Students are more likely to carry and use a book such as this one, for it is small enough to be easily carried and its soft cover is plastic-coated and durable. This is the one book my students carry at all times, even using it to settle arguments in other courses.

3. *Approach.* *Writers INC* is a handbook and all-purpose reference for anyone interested in writing and learning. Using a personal tone and referring directly to the reader as "you" makes it readable. Several colleagues have asked for a copy.

4. *Format.* Bold headings identify concepts. Sections, such as charts, are highlighted for easy location. The sketches are informative as well as humorous. At first, I use worksheets from the publisher familiarizing students with the layout. The table of contents provides page numbers for general headings, and the index lists specific information by topic numbers. This cross-indexing allows easy access to the contents.

5. *Content.* "How can they put so many tomatoes in one little can?" The book is indeed all-purpose containing examples from grammar, punctuation, and spelling. The major portion of the book considers the writing process, from brainstorming to lists of topics, to finished examples of paragraphs, book reviews and research papers, in both MLA and APA styles.

Add cooperative groups, thinking skills, learning styles, reading hints, and literary terms. My favorite feature is the quotes; the students like Frost's, "You can be a little ungrammatical if you come from the right part of the country." The appendix includes tables, maps, and useful lists such as computer terms, presidents, the Constitution, table of the elements, and proofreading symbols. The list of current, useful information goes on and on.

I find myself referring to the book more, teaching some units directly from it, and in other units requiring students to use it independently. In grading papers I refer to item numbers for correcting. Instead of little carryover from year to year, students more readily retain concepts or at least have a source in which to find them.

What do teachers and students say about *Writers INC?*

Writers INC is the best thing that has happened to our English department in a long time! Thank you! Thank you!
—Susan, Georgia

Writers INC is excellent, first class. . . . Former graduates of our high school state that *Writers INC* is better than books that they have had to buy in college. —Phil, Nebraska

Please find enclosed my order for many of your wonderful books. I teach ninth-grade English and find your materials exceedingly efficient and effective. We love the humor and having everything in one place for a quick reference.
—Gloria, Colorado

I would like a hardcover copy of *Writers INC*. I am enclosing a check. A speedy return would be appreciated.

I would also like to add that I bought my first copy of *Writers INC* in high school, a softcover which is so well-worn from over two years of use. I must compliment you, for I found in this book something I could easily use and, at the same time, enjoy reading. It is a practical, brilliant, and fresh approach to writing, learning, and form, one that takes a personal slant toward writing and understands the problems most people face when asked to write a research paper or a poem. It is a book that I am sure to use over and over again in my college career. —Scott, Alabama

Many of you have discovered the wonders of *Basic English Revisited* and found a handbook that your students will actually purchase and use. I've used it for four years because the book so clearly addressed student needs. The bad news is that that book is not going to be available much longer. The good news is that the revision, titled *Writers INC*, has surpassed the original.

For those teachers who have never seen either book, this handbook is truly student-friendly. . . . The Meridian district recently adopted this as a handbook for secondary students. This book is so good students will actually steal it. That's the equivalent of an endorsement.
—From a review,
Idaho Council Teachers
of English Newsletter

I have recently discovered your wonderful publication, *Writers INC*, and have fallen in love with it! What a great source book! As an English and Special Ed. teacher, I am finding it extremely useful in all my classes. Where can I get more? A number of my senior honors students have asked where they could get their own copies, seeing it as a valuable tool for college as well as their remaining time in high school.
—Robert, California

Getting Started . . .

1. Designing Your Own Handbook

Before you even hand out *Writers INC*, ask students what they would put into an all-purpose student handbook if they were in charge of designing one for their school. After students have compiled their lists, go over them in class. Then, hand out copies of *Writers INC*. Have students look through the book and locate as many things as they can from their list. Have them start a second list of items they find in the handbook which they wish they had included in their own.

2. First Impressions

Give students at least 10 minutes to preview *Writers INC*. Then have them write freely for 10 minutes (the focus of their writing being their first impressions) and follow with group and class discussions about their discoveries. What develops is a whole language minilesson.

3. Using the Handbook

After students have gotten a look at *Writers INC*, duplicate and hand out the "Using the Handbook" page in this booklet and work through the table of contents and index information. (You can also refer them to the "Using the Handbook" page in the handbook which shows them even more specifically how the topic numbers work.) Continue the handbook search by giving students the "Handbook Search" pages.

4. Scavenger Hunts

Once students understand how the handbook works, you might experiment with the "Scavenger Hunts" (pp. 82-92). You can also follow the suggestions given there for student-created "hunts."

5. Minilessons

Select a minilesson (or two) from those listed in this teacher's guide (pp. 93-127).

6. Pick 'n Share

Give your students the following assignment: Find one page, one short section, one set of guidelines, one illustration, or one quotation you find interesting, entertaining, stimulating, valuable, etc. (Students should be prepared to share their discoveries.)

7. Clustering to Learn

Develop a cluster with *Writers INC* as the nucleus word. (See page 28 in this book and *clustering* in the handbook.) Follow with a brainstorming session for a group cluster.

8. Why We Write

Read "Why We Write" (p. 1) in *Writers INC* and ask students to free-write for about 5 minutes about something they discovered once when they were writing.

9. Read and React

Have students read any section (1-3 pages) in the handbook and write a brief personal reaction to it.

Using the Handbook

Your handbook is designed to be useful to you not only in your English class, but also as a handy reference book in other classes. It is a basic tool for any writing task from preparing a paper for a health course to taking notes in a geography class, from giving an oral report for a science class to taking an essay test in a history course.

The **Table of Contents** near the front of your handbook gives you a list of the major divisions and the units found under those divisions. It tells you the page number on which each unit begins.

DIRECTIONS: Use the table of contents in your handbook to help you answer the following questions.

1. On which page will you find the start of information about writing summaries?

   _____

2. On which page will you find information on taking tests?

   _____

3. On which page will you find information on marking punctuation?

   _____

4. On which page will you find information on whether to use the term "lady doctor"?

   _____

The **Index** at the back of the handbook is one of its most useful parts. It is similar to the table of contents since it will also help you find things in the handbook. But the index contains much more information. It is arranged in alphabetical order and includes all the important topics discussed in the handbook. The numbers after each word in the index refer to the topic numbers, not the page numbers. Since there are often many topics on one page, these topic numbers will help you to find information more quickly.

DIRECTIONS: Use the index at the back of your handbook to help you answer the following questions.

5. Which topic numbers will help you understand the editorial?

   _____

6. Which topic number will tell you the abbreviation for each state?

   _____

7. Which topic number explains the difference between *biannual* and *biennial*?

   _____

   What is the difference?_____

   _____

8. Which topic number provides an explanation of the amendments of the Constitution?

   _____

   How many amendments are there?

   _____

HANDBOOK SEARCH A
Locating Information

DIRECTIONS: Using your handbook, answer the following questions.

1. What is clustering? _____

   _____

2. What is an analogy? _____

   _____

3. A comma splice is a mistake made when _____

   _____ .

4. What is a red herring? _____

   _____

   _____

5. According to parliamentary procedure, can a
   person interrupt a speaker to amend a motion? _____

6. What are the benefits of keeping a learning log? _____

   _____

   _____

   _____

7. What is another name for the Works Cited section in a research paper? _____

8. What is one use of underlining (italics)? _____

   _____

9. What is the final step in the writing process? _____

10. What does the root *greg* mean? _____

HANDBOOK SEARCH B
Locating Information

DIRECTIONS: Using your handbook, answer the following questions.

1. Are commas used to set off restrictive or nonrestrictive clauses? _____

2. What is a research paper? _____

   _____

3. How many kilometers are there in a mile? _____

4. What is the past tense of the verb *drag?* _____ *bite?* _____

5. Choose the only correctly spelled word from the
   following: *villian, transfered, sincerely,* and *sacriligious.* _____

6. Identify one "don't" for résumé writing. _____

   _____

7. On which planet would you weigh the most? _____

8. Identify one guideline for taking an essay test that you seldom practice. _____

   _____

9. In what class would you most likely be reading
   a book with a Dewey Decimal System number 970? _____

10. Which country has the coordinates 14° N, 89° W? _____

11. Which president served two nonconsecutive terms? _____

12. What does the prefix *retro* mean? _____

13. Irony is _____

14. List three transitions or linking expressions which can be used to conclude or summarize
    a point you are making in your writing.

    _____

HANDBOOK SEARCH C
Getting to Know Your Handbook

DIRECTIONS: Find suitable words to complete the chart below. Be sure the words you select begin with the letters in the left-hand column. Use each word only once. *Note:* **You won't necessarily find a word that corresponds to each letter for all of the categories.**

	Commonly Misspelled Words	Thinking Terms (Page 247)	Computer Terms	Prepositions	Commonly Mixed Pairs (Page 284)	Countries I Have Never Seen	(Your Own Category)
W	weird						
R							
I							
T							
E							
R							
S							
I							
N							
C							

Answers to Using the Handbook
and Handbook Search A, B, & C

1. 104
2. 210
3. 257
4. 12
5. 243, 524
6. 706
7. 729 A biannual event happens twice a year. A biennial event happens every two years.
8. 963, 26 amendments

1. Clustering is a prewriting activity which will help a writer select a writing idea. (See 031.)
2. An analogy is a comparison of two or more similar objects so as to suggest that they are alike in a number of respects. (See 279.)
3. two independent clauses are spliced together with only a comma.
4. A red herring refers to a stinky smoked fish dragged across a trail to throw a tracking dog off the scent. (See 554.)
5. no
6. It gets students actively involved in their course work. And it gives them an opportunity to explore important ideas and concepts presented in the course.
7. bibliography
8. to indicate a foreign word which has not been adopted in the English language (See 658-661.)
9. editing and proofreading
10. herd, group, crowd

1. nonrestrictive clauses
2. A research paper is a documented essay which requires careful planning, searching, studying, and writing.
3. 1.6093 kilometers
4. dragged, bit
5. sincerely
6. Don't emphasize what you want in a job; stress how you fit into the employer's needs. (See 424.)
7. Jupiter
8. (See 475.)
9. history
10. El Salvador
11. Grover Cleveland (See 966.)
12. backwards
13. using a word or phrase to mean the exact opposite of its normal meaning.
14. as a result, finally, in conclusion (See 103.)

Answers will vary.

Writing Programs— Strategies for using *Writers INC*

Contemporary Writing Programs

How were you taught to write?

Did your teachers approach writing as a series of isolated skills that had to be learned sequentially? Did they assign compositions on Mondays with little or no direction and expect flawless finished copies on Fridays? Do either of these approaches sound familiar? They should. For years, teachers used methods like these to "teach" writing. Consider yourself fortunate if you had teachers who provided you with classrooms that were conducive to real writing and learning.

How is writing taught today?

If you are up on your contemporary writing research, you know this isn't an appropriate question. Writing isn't really taught. That is, writing isn't a set of facts, forms, or formulas that a teacher imparts, and it certainly isn't worksheet busywork. We now know that it is (or should be) a student-centered activity that is learned through a variety of shared writing experiences.

So where does this put the teacher?

Not behind his desk lecturing or correcting last night's assignments. It puts him right alongside his students; teachers and students write and learn together. The writing teacher's most important function is to provide the proper mixture of freedom, encouragement, and guidance so that he and his students can learn by doing. He functions much like the understanding parent or a personal mentor.

And if writing is not taught, then how is it learned?

There are a number of contemporary approaches that promote writing as a student-centered learning activity. All of these approaches have a number of things in common in addition to being student centered.

■ **They don't require a textbook.** Most textbooks by their very nature are prescriptive. That is, they are designed as much to tie students and teachers to the textbook program as they are to help students develop as independent thinkers and writers. In a contemporary writing classroom, the students' own writing serves as the textbook. With the support of the necessary reference materials (including a handbook), students and teachers help each other develop and grow as writers.

■ **They require little full-class instruction.** In most contemporary writing classrooms, students work and learn individually and in small groups. Instruction is based on need—when an individual or a group of students need help with a basic skill or rhetorical concept. The form of the instruction is usually a 10-15 minute minilesson. (See p. 93 in this booklet for information on minilessons.) Full-class activities are kept to a minimum so students have as much opportunity as possible to develop their own writing.

■ **They are lively and active.** Modern writing programs promote active learning. On any given day, a student might spend time in a group critiquing session or working on a project of his or her own or helping a classmate sort out a writing problem. There's no hiding in the last row of the classroom as the teacher lectures.

■ **They are well planned.** That contemporary writing programs are student directed doesn't mean that students can simply do as they please. Even the most motivated students will take advantage of too much freedom. Deadlines, support materials, methods of instruction, methods for measuring writing progress, and sensible classroom management procedures all have to be established for a program to be successful. Programs must also be flexible enough to meet the needs and interests of the students (obviously within reason) as the course work progresses.

■ **They are integrated.** That is, writing programs draw from all of the significant research. A particular program won't, for example, be based solely on the writing process approach or on thematic learning. Instead, it will be a blend or incorporation of approaches. (Brief descriptions of six of the most significant approaches to writing follow.)

The Process Approach

In this approach, students learn that writing, real writing, is a process of discovery and exploration rather than an end product or a series of basic skills. As students develop their writing, they address the different steps in the writing process—prewriting, writing the first draft, revising, editing, and proofreading. And the writing they develop, for the most part, stems from their own experiences and thinking.

Students use prewriting activities to discover writing ideas they know and care about. They are encouraged to talk about their ideas and create a community of writers within the classroom. They write first drafts freely, and they revise carefully. After editing and proofreading, students share or publish their work.

Review the section on the writing process (002-036) in *Writers INC* with your students for a more thorough discussion of this approach. (For additional information on the writing process, read Donald Murray's *Learning by Teaching* and *Inside Out* by Dan Kirby and Tom Liner.)

The Writing Workshop Approach

In a writing workshop, students write every day or work on writing-related issues (reading, researching, critiquing, participating in editing sessions, etc.). They are expected to keep all of their work in writing folders, and they are expected to produce a predetermined number of finished pieces by the end of the term. Students are encouraged to take risks, and to experiment with new forms and techniques. Support during each writing project comes from peer and teacher conferences. Students utilize the steps in the writing process to develop their writing.

In a writing workshop, the teacher acts as a guide and facilitator. He or she creates a classroom environment that is conducive to the workshop approach. Desks and chairs are arranged to make student interaction easy. The classroom is stocked with an ample supply of relevant reading and writing materials. Instruction and advice is given when it is needed on an individual basis, in small groups, or to the entire class. The teacher also serves as the final editor before a piece is published.

Make sure to review pages 49-50 in this teacher's guide for more on writing workshops. Also review "Group Advising and Revising" (025) and "Cooperative Group Skills" (465) in *Writers INC* with your students for discussions related to peer conferencing. If you conduct a computer writing lab, refer students to "Writing with a Computer" (173). (For additional information on writing and reading workshops, read *In the Middle* by Nancie Atwell.)

The Thematic Approach

With this approach a teacher (or a team of teachers) chooses a theme *(change, power, courage, speed, etc.)* to serve as the focus for an intense, integrated language experience—that is, an experience which immerses students in integrated reading, writing, listening, and speaking activities as well as activities that may cross curricular boundaries.

If an English teacher plans a thematic unit, he or she will start with a specific theme like *change.* He or she would then select related pieces of literature (tapes, videos, articles, etc.) and various prewriting activities as starting points for the thematic study. Students would then explore *change* from a number of different perspectives and eventually focus their attention on one activity or aspect of the unit to develop into a finished project (an essay, script, presentation, etc.).

If a team of teachers plans a thematic unit together, each instructor determines how to address the theme in his or her discipline. Some themes will lend themselves to a great deal of carryover or cross-pollination among the disciplines, and other themes may not. Regardless, the point is to get as many disciplines as possible working together to create a meaningful "thematic" learning experience for the students. (Refer to *Restructuring for an Interdisciplinary Curriculum,* edited by John M. Jenkins and Daniel Turner [NASSP] for more information.)

The Personal Experience Approach

The focus of this approach is simple: students enjoy writing and find it meaningful if it stems from their personal experiences and observations. Students usually keep a journal in an experiential program, so they have a number of potential writing ideas to draw from. As with most contemporary approaches, the writing process and some form of a writing workshop are incorporated into the program.

James Moffett in his *Active Voices* series [Heinemann] outlines a schoolwide program stemming from experiential writing. The assignments in his program progress from very personal types of writing to more remote and complex types of writing. It follows that the more students write experientially, the better able they are to address increasingly more complex experiences in more sophisticated forms of writing. (See pp. 129-145 in this teacher's guide for a preview of the *Writers File* writing program based on Moffett's experiential approach. This program coordinates with *Writers INC*.)

> *"[Active Voices] is not a particular approach based on writing 'exercises' ... In fact, it challenges such an approach and insists that only within some whole actual discourse based on individual thinking can words, sentences, and paragraphs be meaningfully practiced and examined."*
> — James Moffett

Author and teacher Ken Macrorie outlines his successful experience-based writing programs in *Writing to Be Read* and *The I-Search Paper* [Heinemann]. Both books help students write honestly and sincerely about their personal experiences. And they help students get a feel for what it takes to produce writing that readers will find interesting and entertaining. Free writing (rapid writing, spontaneous writing) plays an integral part in Macrorie's approach to writing. In *The I-Search Paper,* he also describes a stimulating approach to research which is based on the students' personal researching experiences.

(See pp. 48-49 in this teacher's guide to learn about our own experience with a personalized approach to writing.)

Contemporary Approaches to Prewriting and Invention

Most writing teachers and researchers would agree that exploring a potential writing idea—that is, getting a feel for it and seeing what it has to offer you and your readers—is perhaps the most critical step in the writing process. At least one third of a writer's time should be devoted to this initial exploration and development.

For many years, free writing, brainstorming (listing), and journal keeping were the basic prewriting techniques available to student writers. But with the work of writers and researchers like Ann Berthoff, Peter Elbow, and Gabriele Rico, among others, students now can choose from a greater number of techniques used to explore potential writing subjects.

Review the "Guidelines for Selecting a Subject" (031) and the "Guidelines for Searching and Shaping a Subject" (033) in *Writers INC* with your students. These guidelines list a number of valuable prewriting techniques. Pay special attention to clustering, cubing, imaginary dialogues, structured questions, and offbeat questions.

> *"We do not write to be understood, we write in order to understand."*
> — C. Day-Lewis

Writing to Learn Across the Curriculum

Writing to learn isn't an additional approach for composition teachers. Rather, it is a method of learning which can (and should) be incorporated across the curriculum. This approach helps students personalize learning so that they understand their course work better and retain what they have learned longer. It also encourages high-level thinking skills.

Teachers need only identify the "language components" in their subjects and select writing-to-learn activities which will most effectively foster thinking and learning. More information about writing to learn is provided on the following page and on pages 70-75. Also, read and discuss "Writing to Learn" (469) in *Writers INC* with your students.

Setting Up a Schoolwide Writing Program

"The productive use of language, and especially writing, is a valuable tool for learning for all students in all subjects at all ages."
— John S. Mayher, Nancy Lester, and Gordon M. Pradl

Understanding the Purpose

Journal writing, dialogues, and stories— these particular forms of writing have traditionally been associated exclusively with the English curriculum. But not any longer. There are more and more teachers in all content areas who have their students explore their thoughts and feelings in journals, confront challenging ideas in dialogues, and develop content-related fictional pieces. And why so?

These teachers realize that writing plays a central role in the learning process. Writing by its very nature gets students actively and thoughtfully involved in their work no matter if they are studying algebraic equations, photosynthesis, or local government. It helps them understand and remember important concepts. It makes them more appreciative of course content and curious to learn more. And it gives students control over their own learning. (Not a bad set of circumstances, is it?)

The Ultimate Learning Tool

Writing is such an important learning tool that all teachers must make room for it in their curriculum. The critical question no longer is *why* students should be writing, but rather how much writing they should be doing and in what forms. That's why we developed this section.

We can think of no better way for all teachers to pool their efforts than to promote writing and learning. It is a no-lose situation. The more proficient students become as writers, the more able they are to learn. We agree with Nancie Atwell's statement in *Coming to Know* (Heinemann, 1990): "In the best of all possible worlds, language study should be part and parcel of the entire school curriculum. The whole school day should be a learning workshop."

Identifying the Basic Types of Writing

There are many reasons for asking students to write; the four reasons that follow deserve attention in any schoolwide writing program:

■ **Writing to Learn** As was mentioned earlier on this page and on the preceding page, writing to better understand or learn new concepts is one of the most beneficial reasons to have students write. It is also the easiest type of writing to implement. (Refer to "Writing to Learn" in this teacher's guide for a list of easy-to-implement writing-to-learn activities.)

■ **Journal Writing** Writing to explore personal thoughts and feelings in a journal works as well in social studies or science as it does in language arts. Students who engage in journal writing become much more in tune with their course work and much more comfortable with the act of composing. (See "A Closer Look at Journal Writing" on p. 45 in this section for more information.)

■ **Writing to Share** Writing to share learning also plays an important part in a schoolwide writing program. Students approach writing with more interest, care, and concern if they know that they have an interested audience with whom to share their work. In the process of sharing their ideas, students naturally learn from one another. (See "A Closer Look at Writing to Share" on p. 45 in this section for more information.)

■ **Writing to Show Learning** Writing to show learning is the traditional reason teachers have had their students write. When students compose summary paragraphs, draft reports, or answer essay test questions, they are writing to show learning. While writing to show learning was once the primary reason to have students write, it is now only one of many reasons to initiate writing.

> *"If the writer does not feel that through writing he will discover something which is uniquely his, he may soon concentrate on craft rather than content and speak with tricks rather than with truth."*
>
> — Donald Murray

Establishing a Planning Framework

What do you need to know about writing to establish a schoolwide writing program? The following recommendations are based on information in *A Guide to Curriculum Planning in English/Language Arts* (Wisconsin Department of Instruction, 1986).

- Curriculum and instruction in writing should reflect the knowledge that we learn language holistically, through whole problems in creating meaning, rather than through practice in isolated skills.
- Writing should be a schoolwide activity, integrated into content-area learning at all levels.
- Texts should reinforce and support teaching that has already gone on within the writing and learning process.
- Students at all levels should engage in original writing every week, gaining consistent experience in working through the entire writing process (prewriting, writing, revising, editing, . . .).
- Teachers should view writing as a developmental process that promotes risk taking and leads to discoveries rather than an accumulation of skills.
- "Basic writing skills" should be taught as much as possible in the context of actual communication.
- Instruction should recognize the contributions of current research in writing and in effective classroom practices.
- Each school (district) should develop a consistent philosophy for the teaching of writing.
- A curriculum based on the writing and learning process sets its own goals and priorities rather than yielding to those set by publishers of textbooks and tests.

Establishing the Proper Classroom Environment

How can teachers create the proper environment for meaningful writing experiences in their classrooms? (Many of the following ideas are based on information provided in *Investigate Nonfiction* by Donald Graves [Heinemann, 1989].)

- Allow students to work on their writing in class. Students need sustained periods of time to immerse themselves in their work.
- Share writing samples so students can see how other students and professionals have written about literature, math, science, history, and so on. (Spend some time discussing these samples to ensure that students fully appreciate the writing.)
- Encourage students to use prewriting activities to discover subjects they know about or are interested in.
- Expect students to write for real audiences—usually their peers—rather than for their teachers or some unknown "other."
- Have students focus on their ideas during early drafts. They should think as they go along, crossing out, switching directions, writing freely, leaving blank spaces and so on.
- Reserve class time for sharing sessions. When students have opportunities to talk about their writing in progress, they generally put more effort into their work.
- Encourage (or require) students to keep track of their writing progress, perhaps in a journal or in a learning log.
- Expect students to revise their writing (adding, cutting, rearranging, and reworking) until it says exactly what they want it to say. They also should be expected to carefully edit and proofread their work.
- Provide encouragement throughout the writing process. (Writing is hard work, and students need to know that someone is there to help them.)
- Have students publish their finished products—which might simply mean that their writing is displayed for their peers to read.

A Closer Look at Journal Writing

Because journal writing binds content (facts, figures, times, places, formulas) together with student feelings (reactions, wonderings, questions), it plays a significant role in making learning happen. Journal writing allows students to immerse themselves intellectually and emotionally in their learning. It allows students to make personal connections with their course work, and it allows them to do so free from the gravitational pull of right answers and performance scores. It provides a way for students to work things out for themselves, to take an active role in their own learning.

Students need only a notebook, a ready supply of pens, and encouragement to write. (Ideally, the notebook will be reserved for journal writing and will not be used elsewhere.) *Writers INC* offers students a good deal of information and ideas to get them started. (See "Journal Writing" and "Learning Logs.") To get students off on the right foot, teachers should ask them to write in their journals on a regular basis, perhaps two or three times a week, for at least 10 minutes at a crack. Students will also need to know that they have the freedom to write about anything on their minds that is somehow related to their course work.

Special Note: Teachers who work with journals often provide one or two prompts each time they have their students write. Students are encouraged to use one of the prompts as a starting point for their writing if they need to, or they can write about a topic of their own choosing. (Why prompts? Teachers can't expect students to have relevant topics in mind every time they write.)

A Closer Look at Writing to Share

Traditionally teachers have relied on very basic forms of writing for assignments—primarily paragraphs, reports, and basic essays. There's nothing wrong with this standard fare, but there are so many other (and better) ways for students to shape their ideas related to their course work. They can write fiction, news stories, feature articles, editorials, letters, manuals, scripts, and so on.

Me, a Writing Expert?

Teachers don't have to be accomplished fiction writers, journalists, or technical writers to bring these different forms of writing into their classrooms. The role of teachers should be to help students develop their thoughts. The teachers are the experts in their respective areas of instruction, and they can put this expertise to good use by guiding students as they select, investigate, and work with writing ideas. By helping students with the ideas of their writing, teachers are serving their students well. When it comes to shaping and refining their writing, the student handbook can provide most of the needed writing, revising, and proofreading guidelines.

Our Recommendations

Why do we recommend that teachers vary the types of writing they assign? If all we ever ate for lunch were ham and cheese sandwiches, we would soon lose our taste for them. The same holds true for writing. You can't expect students to have much of an appetite for writing if their diet never varies.

But there is another reason. Assigning paragraphs and reports generally promotes what James Britton calls "classificatory writing—or writing which reflects information in the form teachers and textbooks present it." Or put in another way, the paragraphs and reports students write often reflect what they have been told or what they have read. The writing reflects little personal thought and, therefore, little learning.

What's needed are opportunities for students to write in more creative and critical ways. Generally speaking, writing letters, editorials, plays, and stories are much more thoughtful enterprises than writing basic paragraphs and reports. These alternative forms demand more commitment on the part of students and get them more intellectually and emotionally involved in their writing. They force students to understand and apply information rather than simply restate it.

As stated earlier, students also need every opportunity to write for real audiences, to write for someone other than their teachers. Writing letters (to send), editorials (to submit), stories (to read to actual audiences), and plays (to perform) provide such opportunities. When students know that there is a real audience out there, they are more apt to put forth their best efforts. Their writing is a reflection of their very own thinking. It only makes sense that they would want it to reflect as positive an image as possible. (See "Designing Writing Assignments" on the following page for information related to writing for real audiences and purposes.)

Designing Writing Assignments

The following discussion will help teachers design meaningful writing assignments, ones that promote writing as a meaning-making process?

Writing Assignment:

In a paragraph, identify three ways in which consumers can produce less waste.

Discussion: It's a sure bet that students' responses to such an assignment will be very predictable . . . and, unfortunately, very dull. ("There are three main ways to cut down on consumer waste. . . .") The assignment follows the age-old formula: question and answer, tell and retell, stimulus and response, fill in the blank. It is limited in scope and intent. It requires little genuine thinking on the part of students, and, therefore, they gain very little from the experience. A meaningful and memorable learning experience it is not. Compare this assignment with the one that follows.

Writing Assignment:

Convince a friend, parent, or neighbor—real or imagined—that he or she should produce less waste.

Subject: The problem of consumer waste

Audience: The subject of your writing and your reading audience (your writing group or classmates)

Purpose: To convince someone to change his or her behavior

Form: Friendly letter, editorial letter, modern fable . . .

Speaker: You, as a young person concerned about the environment

Guidelines for Evaluation:
- Does the writing sound convincing? (Are main points supported by specific details?)
- Does the writing form a meaningful whole, moving smoothly and clearly from one point to the next?
- Will readers appreciate the treatment of this assignment?

Discussion: So many more possibilities are presented to students in the second example. They can't follow a formula or simply repeat what they have already been told or what they have already read. Instead, they have to apply their knowledge about the subject matter in a specific context which they help to design. They have to decide who they are going to address, what they are going to say, and how they are going to say it. It is the type of assignment that can lead to real learning.

Getting Started

In *Learning to Write/Writing to Learn* (Heinemann-Boynton/Cook, 1983), authors John Mayher, Nancy Lester, and Gordon Pradl provide a basic, three-step process to help teachers develop well-conceived writing assignments.

- First, teachers should define or identify learning objectives in their disciplines that could be facilitated by writing. The authors stress that these must be genuine objectives (to help students relate the problem of consumer waste to their immediate world, for instance) rather than activities.
- They should then design a writing assignment which would help students achieve a specified objective.
- Lastly, teachers should establish guidelines or criteria to evaluate the outcome of the students' work. (Evaluation should focus on writing as a process of exploring and shaping.)

Special Note: A planning sheet is provided on the next page to help teachers design well-conceived writing assignments.

What to Consider

When designing a writing task, consider the following: A meaningful writing assignment . . .
- ❏ places students at the center of the writing and learning process,
- ❏ evolves either from general instruction or prewriting activities,
- ❏ is clearly described to the students,
- ❏ directly or indirectly addresses all five elements of effective communication (subject, audience, purpose, form, speaker),
- ❏ and offers options for the students.

Assignment Planning Sheet

SUBJECT:

AUDIENCE:

PURPOSE:

FORM:

SPEAKER:

* * * * * * * * * * * * * * *

PREWRITING ACTIVITIES: (Prewriting activities are important if the writing assignment does not stem from information or concepts already covered in the class.)

1.

2.

GUIDELINES FOR EVALUATION: (Emphasize clarity, inventiveness, and depth of thought more than correctness.)

1.

2.

3.

Implementing an Experience-Based Writing Program

"I can tap into [my students'] human instincts to write if I help them realize that their lives and memories are worth telling stories about, and if I help them zoom in on topics of fundamental importance to them."
— writing teacher June Gould

We know from firsthand experience that the personal stories students love to share can serve as the basis of an effective and lively writing program. Here's how our program worked.

Getting Started

At the beginning of the school year, we introduced in-class journal writing to the students. (We encouraged students to write outside of class in journals as well, but the journals in school were part of our writing program.) We knew that the most effective way to get students into writing was simply to let them write often and freely about their own lives, without having to worry about grades or turning their writing in. This helped them develop a feel for writing, real writing, writing that originated from their own thoughts and feelings.

Hint We provided our students with four or five personal writing prompts each time they wrote. They could use one of these prompts as a starting point for their writing if they wished. The choice was theirs. (We found that providing writing prompts was much easier and more productive than going into our "You've got plenty to write about" song and dance.)

Writing Prompts

Here's a typical list of one day's writing prompts: Write about

- your most uncomfortable social experience,
- coping with younger brothers or sisters,
- being out, late at night,

- or what you did over the past weekend.

(See 034 in the handbook for lists of writing prompts.)

We would ask our students to write every other day for the first 10 minutes of the class period. Students knew that every Monday, Wednesday, and Friday were writing days. Of course, we had to adjust our schedule at times, but, for the most part, we tried to stick to writing every other day.

Keeping It Going

After everyone was seated and roll was taken, the journals were passed out, the prompts were given, and everyone wrote. We expected students to write for the complete 10 minutes nonstop. And we made sure that they did. They knew that they would be given a quarter journal grade for the number of words they produced. This almost made a contest out of the writing sessions. Each time they wrote, they wanted to see if they could increase their production from past journal entries, and they always wanted to write more than their classmates. (As they were doing this, they were becoming increasingly more fluent as writers.)

Wrapping It Up

On days that they weren't writing, students were reacting to each other's journal entries. Each student first exchanged his or her entry with a classmate. They then counted the words in their partner's work. Afterwards, they reread the entry and made comments on things they liked or questioned in the writing. The students spent a few minutes discussing each other's writing; then the class as a whole particiated in a sharing session.

Many students were reluctant to share their own entries with the entire class. But they had no problem reading their partner's entry ("You've got to hear Nick's story"). The students loved listening and reacting to these shared entries.

Personal Experience Papers

Periodically, we would interrupt the normal course of journal writing and sharing and make formal writing assignments. That is, we would ask students to review their entries and select one (or part of one) to develop into a more polished, complete personal experience paper. Those entries that readers enjoyed and wanted to know more about would usually be the ones the students would choose to develop.

We wanted to make sure that their writing went through at least one or two thorough revisions, so we gave our writers plenty of class time to work on their papers. They also were required to turn in all of their preliminary work with their final drafts.

The experience papers were shared with the entire class at the end of the project. This was an informal activity, but one that students came to appreciate as an important part of the entire composing process. It was their day. They were on stage. They were sharing the end product of all of their work.

Implementing a Writing Workshop

In a writing workshop, the primary focus during each class period is to provide students with a large block of time to work on writing projects of their choice. At least 30 minutes should be reserved for writing or a writing-related activity such as researching, conferencing, or publishing. Many teachers also reserve time for minilessons (5-10 minutes), status checks to keep track of the students' work (2-3 minutes), and sharing sessions (5 minutes). *Note:* For some minilessons a teacher might require that all students participate in the work. For other ones, only certain students may be required to participate, depending on the needs of the students and the subject of the minilesson.

Instructor's Role

The teacher serves as a facilitator making sure that his or her classroom is conducive to writing, conferencing, reading, and researching. He or she also serves as a writing mentor helping each student make the most out of each writing project.

There's a direct correlation between the effectiveness of a writing workshop and the effectiveness of a teacher's record keeping and planning. A workshop facilitator must make sure that important concepts are covered, essential skills are taught, and each student's progress is charted during the course of each grading period. This can only be accomplished through careful planning and record keeping. Status-of-the-class sheets, daily work charts, conference checklists, and semester evaluation forms are just a few of the many forms that can help teachers manage a workshop. (Teachers who are interested in implementing a writing workshop in their classrooms should contact the Write Source for a packet containing a variety of handy workshop checklists and forms. Ask for Mary or Dave.)

Student's Role

Students should come to each workshop session with their writing folders intact, containing all drafts of their works in progress. (A student's writing folder is his or her text for the class.) They should also have a plan of action in mind for each session (that plan should obviously include some form of writing). A student's success or failure in a workshop depends on his or her ability to manage time effectively and turn the required work in on time. As a result, they should always be aware of established due dates and deadlines.

Students should also expect to share their writing, offer advice to their writing colleagues, and generally conduct themselves maturely and cooperatively. Finished pieces of writing should reflect a student's best efforts after careful revising, editing, and proofreading. At the end of a grading period, students should compile the required number of finished pieces in a portfolio for evaluation.

Special Note: On the following page, you will find a basic weekly schedule for a writing workshop. This schedule can serve as a starting point for planning. Individual teachers will definitely want to make adjustments to meet the specific needs in their classrooms.

Writing Workshop: Weekly Schedule

This schedule can vary depending on the teacher's needs. One teacher might, for example, conduct writing workshops for three days a week and reading workshops for the other two days. Another teacher might vary the regular routine from time to time and conduct extended lessons dealing with important writing skills. Then again, a teacher might conduct minilessons two or three days a week and have students write in a journal or work on daily language activities on the other days.

Monday	Tuesday	Wednesday	Thursday	Friday
Writing Minilesson #5 10 MIN.	**Writing Minilesson #6** 10 MIN.	**Writing Minilesson #7** 10 MIN.	**Writing Minilesson #8** 10 MIN.	**Quiz or Review Minilesson #5 - #8** 10 MIN.
Status Check 2 MIN. (Find out what students will work on for the day.)	**Status Check** 2 MIN.	**Status Check** 2 MIN.	**Status Check** 2 MIN.	**Status Check** 2 MIN.
Individual Work Writing, Revising, Editing, Conferencing, or Publishing 30 MIN.	**Individual Work** Writing, Revising, Editing, Conferencing, or Publishing 30 MIN.	**Individual Work** Writing, Revising, Editing, Conferencing, or Publishing 30 MIN.	**Individual Work** Writing, Revising, Editing, Conferencing, or Publishing 30 MIN.	**Individual Work** Writing, Revising, Editing, Conferencing, or Publishing 30 MIN.
Whole Class Sharing Session 5 MIN.	**Whole Class Sharing Session** 5 MIN.	**Whole Class Sharing Session** 5 MIN.	**Whole Class Sharing Session** 5 MIN.	**Whole Class Sharing Session** 5 MIN.

Evaluating Student Writing

"If any man wishes to write in a clear style, let him first be clear in his thoughts."
— Johann Wolfgang von Goethe

Teachers need to practice two different types of evaluation when they respond to student writing: **formative evaluation** (evaluating while the student is forming the project) and **summative evaluation** (evaluating the total outcome, or sum, of the student's effort). Formative evaluation does not result in a grade; summative evaluation does. Some teachers do choose, however, to give students a set number of points (a performance score) during different stages in the formative steps in the writing process.

Formative Evaluation

Formative evaluation is most often used for writing-to-learn activities, prewriting activities, writing in progress, journal entries, and so forth. Four types of formative evaluation are widely used:

- Desk-side conference
- Scheduled teacher/student conference
- Written questions and responses
- Peer responses

Note: Make sure your students understand writing as a process. Review "The Writing Process" in the *Writers INC* handbook when and if necessary.

DESK-SIDE CONFERENCES occur when a teacher stops at a student's desk to ask questions and make responses while students are working. In the early stages of the writing process, responses and questions should be about writing ideas, content, audience, purpose, generating ideas, and getting those ideas on paper. Questions should be open-ended. This gives the writer "space" to talk. When a writer is talking, he is thinking, clarifying, and making decisions. Teachers should not attempt to solve problems for the students, but instead ask questions and suggest possible solutions.

Respond to a student's paper as a reader, not as a teacher. Address underdevelopment, the most common problem young writers face in the first stages of the writing process. Also see the PQS conference format discussed in the next column.

SCHEDULED TEACHER/STUDENT CONFERENCES provide opportunities for students to initiate conferences with you. Student/teacher conferences usually take one of three forms:

- ❑ Student-directed conference
- ❑ PQS conference
- ❑ Small group conference

A student-directed conference may occur when a student has finished a rough draft or a final draft, has identified a problem or need, wishes to establish new criteria for his/her next project, or wishes to share a breakthrough, a success, a "good thing."

A PQS conference (praise-P, question-Q, and suggest-S) will help you refrain from dominating the conference or overteaching. A typical conference lasts from 3 to 5 minutes. First, offer specific and honest praise. Second, ask an appropriate question (one that relates to the writing stage the student is in and one that prompts student talking). Last, offer one or two suggestions.

Small group conferences may be groups of three to five students who are at the same stage of the writing process or are experiencing the same problem. The goal of a small group conference is twofold: first, to help students improve their writing and second, to help students develop as evaluators of writing.

 Hint Build a portfolio of student revising samples. Include before and after passages. "Label" these samples and put them in a binder students can refer to whenever they need help with their writing.

WRITTEN QUESTIONS AND RESPONSES help a teacher vary her evaluating techniques, supplement desk-side conferencing, and provide a lasting record.

Collect works in progress. Write comments similar to those you use in conferences and ask open-ended questions so students can actively seek solutions.

In the editing and proofreading stage you can ask, "Why do you need a comma here?" Students must answer the questions and correct the errors. However, with inexperienced writers it is best not to mark all of the errors. Draw a double line to indicate where you stopped marking errors.

Students learn just as much from what they are doing right as they do from what they are doing wrong. Make positive comments! Identify good things!

"At first, I thought, 'Why bother?' What did we know about writing? I resented the group discussions about my writing and offered very few suggestions. Later I realized that we were talking about what we each need right now, for this paper. That was something even a teacher couldn't tell me."
— Paul, a student

PEER RESPONSES Students can become expert responders, but you must train them. You have already begun to do this in both desk-side and scheduled conferences.

Provide some guide sheets or forms for students to use in peer conferences. (See 029 in *Writers INC* for a sample checklist.) It is best if students work in pairs and have a very limited agenda. Always model how to use the form for your entire class. Impose a time limit to keep students on task (15-20 minutes).

One very simple process to use for peer advising is to ask a student to read his partner's paper and then generate three questions beginning with *who, what, where, when, why,* or *how.* The questions and paper are returned to the writer who responds to these questions. These questions serve as a starting point for a discussion. You can use more elaborate processes as students become better peer responders. (See "Group Advising and Revising" in *Writers INC* for more information.)

Summative Evaluation

Summative evaluation produces a grade and is used for final papers and projects. Once you assign a grade, the student interprets this as a signal that this piece of writing is finished. We want our students to value the learning process as much if not more than the final product, and we want their attention on personal goals, not grades.

However, the day will come when we must assign a grade. Here are some general principles to help you do that:

1. Clearly establish the criteria for each piece of writing or for each student. Limit the criteria so you do not overwhelm the student or yourself. Establishing criteria for each student during a personal conference will allow you to fit the criteria to the student and his/her learning task.

2. Ask students to help you develop the criteria. This can be done in personal conferences or with the whole class. Students readily accept and understand criteria they have helped build.

3. Students must have ample opportunities for formative evaluation before their final product receives a grade. Students deserve points for the work they have done during the writing process.

4. Concern for content, fluency, and fresh ideas should be of primary concern during summative evaluation for young writers. Mechanical correctness will follow fluency. As students gain control of their language, their errors decrease.

5. Students should be involved in the summative evaluation. A form which asks them to circle the best parts of their writing, list the problems they encountered, draw a squiggly line around parts they would work on if they had more time, and write down the suggestions they tried gives students input. In addition to the above information, they should be asked how much time they put into a project and what grade they would give themselves.

6. You will be very familiar with the piece of writing because of the formative evaluations. You may choose one of the systems that follows to establish a grade.

Approaches for Evaluating Writing

Analytic Scales establish the features necessary for a successful piece of writing and attribute point values for each feature. The grade derives from the point total. Many students like this form of evaluation because it is concrete, and it highlights specific strengths and weaknesses in their writing. The emphasis of analytic scales tends, however, to be on the parts rather than the whole.

Holistic Grading evaluates a piece of writing as a whole. The most basic approach to holistic grading is to read the paper rather quickly for a general impression. The paper is graded according to this impression. A reader might also compare a particular piece with a number of pieces already graded, or grade it for the appearance of elements important to that type of writing. Holistic grading helps teachers reward creativity, inventiveness, and overall effect.

Task-Specific Scoring accords a grade based on how well a student has accomplished specific rhetorical tasks. A teacher might, for example, create a scoring checklist or guide for a short fiction writing assignment. This checklist would include those elements that are inherent in this writing form—plot, characterization, point of view, etc. Students must understand the criteria for scoring before they begin their writing. This type of grading addresses specific rather than open-ended writing assignments.

Portfolio Grading gives students an opportunity to choose pieces of writing to be graded. This is a common method of evaluation in writing workshops. Workshop students compile all of their work in a portfolio or folder. Teachers require them to submit a specified number of finished projects for grading each quarter or semester. Students enjoy this method of evaluation because it gives them some control over the evaluation process; teachers like it because they don't have to grade everything a student has written, and this lessens their work load.

A Performance System is a quick and simple method of evaluation. If students complete a writing activity and it meets the previously established level of acceptability, they receive the pre-established grade or points for completing the assignment. The student either has completed the activity or he hasn't. (This method works well for evaluating journals.)

Responding to Student Writing

The following guidelines will help you assess nongraded and graded writing. (Nongraded writing refers to writing in progress and writing-to-learn activities.)

Responding to Nongraded Writing (Formative)

- Discard your red pens and pencils. Use a #2 pencil when responding to student writing.
- Clarify criteria for evaluation. Make the criteria known in advance.
- Scan the writing once quickly. Ask the question, "Has the student understood and responded appropriately to the activity?"
- Reread the writing and indicate that it has or has not fulfilled the requirements of the activity. You may choose to place a check mark on the front page, write a summary sentence on the last page, and/or note areas needing further attention.
- Respond noncritically. Use positive, supportive language.
- Use marginal dialogue. Resist writing on or over the student's writing.
- Underline points you wish to highlight, question, or confirm. Never circle, cross out, or otherwise undermine the student's writing.
- Whenever possible, respond in the form of questions.
- Encourage risk taking.

Evaluating Graded Writing (Summative)

- Have students submit prewriting and rough drafts with their final drafts.
- Scan final drafts once, focusing on the writing as a whole.
- Read it again, this time evaluating it for its adherence to previously established criteria.
- As you read the draft a second time, make marginal notations. Be sure the notations address the process as you evaluate the product. Use supportive language.
- Scan the writing a third and final time. Write a summary comment on the last page of the student's writing.
- Assign a grade. Remember that you are evaluating both process and product.

Using Writing Portfolios

More and more, English teachers are making portfolios an important part of their writing programs. Will portfolios work for you? Will they help you and your students assess their writing? Read on and find out.

What is a writing portfolio?

A writing portfolio is a limited collection of a student's writing for evaluation. A portfolio is different from the traditional writing folder. A writing folder (also known as a working folder) contains all of a student's work; a portfolio contains only a student's best efforts.

Why should I ask students to compile writing portfolios?

Having students compile portfolios makes the whole process of writing so much more meaningful to them. They will more willingly put forth their best efforts as they work on various writing projects, knowing that they are accountable for producing a certain number of finished pieces for publication. They will more thoughtfully approach writing as an involved and recursive process of drafting, sharing, and rewriting, knowing that this process leads to more effective writing. And they will more responsibly craft finished pieces, knowing that their final evaluation depends on the finished products they include in their portfolios.

Any or all methods of assessment can be employed when portfolios are used, including self-evaluation, peer evaluation, contract writing, traditional grading, and so on. (For more on assessment, refer to pp. 51-53 in this teacher's guide.)

How many pieces of writing should be included in a portfolio?

Although you and your students will best be able to decide this, we advise that students compile at least three or four pieces of writing in a portfolio each quarter. (Students could contract for a certain amount of required writing.) All of the drafts should be included for each piece. Students should also be required to include a reflective writing or self-critique sheet that assesses their writing progress.

Special Note: Some teachers allow students to include one or two pieces of writing from other disciplines in their portfolios.

When do portfolios work best?

Students need plenty of class time to work on writing if they are going to produce effective portfolios. If they are used right, portfolios turn reluctant writers into practicing writers. And practicing writers need regularly scheduled blocks of time to "practice" their craft, to think, talk, and explore options in their writing over and over again.

How can I help my students with their portfolio writing?

Allow students to explore topics of genuine interest to them. Also allow them to write for many different purposes and audiences and in many different forms.

In addition, expect students to evaluate their own writing and the writing of their peers as it develops—and help them to do so. (See "Group Advising and Revising" in the handbook for help.) Provide them with sound guidance when they need help with a writing problem. And create a classroom environment that encourages students to immerse themselves in writing.

How do I grade a portfolio?

Base each grade on goals you and your students establish at the beginning of the grading period and on what is achieved as evidenced in the portfolio. Many teachers develop a critique sheet for assessment that is based on the goals established by the class. (It's critical that students know how many pieces they should include in their portfolios, how their work should be arranged in their portfolios, how the portfolios will be assessed, and so on.)

"Portfolios have become each student's story of who they are as readers and writers, rich with the evidence of what they are able to do and how they are able to do it."
— Linda Rief

What About Grammar?

Grammar, to our way of thinking, relates to those features of the language that are used by speakers of the standard dialect. We do not look at it as a traditional course of study in which rules and isolated sentence analysis and sentence diagramming are emphasized. Rather, we see it as best taught in the context of the student's own work. What follows is a list of classroom practices which promote meaningful context-based grammar instruction, mixed with occasional minilessons and other daily language activities.

Promoting Meaningful Grammar Instruction

- Approach grammar as an essential element in the development of effective writing. Link grammar as much as possible to the student's own writing.

- Make editing and proofreading of the student's writing an important part of classroom work. Students should have ready access to a resource for their proofreading. ("Remarks" in *Writers INC* [600-945] will answer any questions students might have.) They should also have practice editing and proofreading cooperatively.

- Instruction should be given in the form of 10-15 minute minilessons. No one should have to sit through period-long lectures on grammar or work on extensive grammar assignments. (See pp. 93-127 in your booklet for minilesson ideas.)

- Help students "hear" punctuation by relating it to pitch, stress, and pause.

- Immerse students in all aspects of language learning: reading, writing, speaking, listening, and thinking. Putting language to good use comes from using language, in all of its forms, on a regular basis.

Approaches That Work

Sentence combining–Use the student's own writing as much as possible. The rationale behind combining ideas and the proper punctuation for combining should be stressed. (Have students refer to 058-082, 102, and 893-919 in *Writers INC* for help.)

Sentence expansion and revising–Give students practice adding and changing information in sentences they have already created. (Refer to 058-082.)

Sentence modeling–Students should have practice imitating writing models. According to James Moffett, this activity is a great teacher of grammer because it exposes young writers to the many possibilities of English grammar beyond the basic forms. (See the sample "Sentence Modeling" activities from the *Writers File* program on p. 141 in this teacher's guide.)

Sentence transforming–Students should practice changing sentences from one form to another (from passive to active, beginning a sentence in a different way, using a different form of a particular word, etc.). (Refer to 058-082.)

- **Daily Language Practice**–Use daily oral language activities to introduce or clarify common student problems with grammar and usage. (Then use actual student samples as needed.) Correct and discuss the problems orally so that students hear as well as see how grammar works. (See a sampler of our daily language practice activities from the *Writers File* program on p. 141 in this teacher's guide.)

Approaches to Avoid

Sentence diagramming–Traditional diagrams as well as transformational or tree diagrams do not improve the students' ability to edit and proofread their own language use.

Labeling–Analyzing and labeling parts of the sentence offer little or no carryover to the students' own work.

Memorizing–Memorizing abstract rules and definitions also provides little or no carryover to the students' own writing.

Identifying mistakes–Having students identify mistakes or make choices on worksheets does little more than keep students busy, unless you immediately apply the lesson to their own writing.

Language and Learning Strategies

Reading: Getting Students to Like It Again

"The best effect of any book is that it excites the reader to self-activity."
—Thomas Carlyle

English teachers, at least those of us who are hooked on books, know exactly what Carlyle means. A good book stimulates us, it moves us emotionally and intellectually, it triggers our imaginations, it enriches our lives. Good books are what made most of us become English teachers in the first place. We wanted to share our enthusiasm about literature and reading with our students.

It didn't take many of us long, however, to discover that getting students excited about literature was extremely difficult, no matter what the book. They liked most of the standard fare all right. Modern titles like *To Kill a Mockingbird* and *Lord of the Flies* were always well received as were some classics like *Huckleberry Finn* and *1984*. But most students didn't become *excited* by them—at least, not in the way that we had envisioned.

Part of the problem has been our approach.

Many of us, quite frankly, have beaten good books into the ground with study guide sheets; check quizzes; plot, character, and thematic analyses; writing projects; and final exams covering everything. We've shared some stimulating moments with our students during the reading, but, for the most part, we haven't given them the opportunity to become excited about literature.

Why did this happen?

Probably because this is how books were presented to us as secondary and university students. The primary purpose of modern literary study has been the detailed and objective analysis of a piece of literature. Little wonder students have reacted so indifferently to reading and literature. We've taken the heart and soul out of the reading process by making it so analytical, so scientific, so academic.

How do we get literature students to share our enthusiasm?

How can we "excite them to self-activity"? Clearly, we must change the focus of our literary study. We can't expect students to share our literary enthusiasm if we don't allow them to meet a good book on their own terms—that is, if we don't give them opportunities to honestly react to and interact with the literature. In *Literature as Exploration*, Louise Rosenblatt states, "The primary subject matter for the reader is the web of feelings, sensations, images, and ideas that he weaves between himself and the text."

". . . this approach makes it possible to enlarge students' understanding of their own behavior and thereby motivate them to read carefully on their own without external threat."
— David Bleich

How do we help students meet good books on their own terms?

We make literature much more student directed, and we do this by . . .

■ providing plenty of sustained reading time for our students without the specter of study guide sheets haunting them. At least one full class period per week should be devoted to reading. If students are given opportunities to lose themselves in good books in school, they will be more willing to read outside of class and more apt to make reading an important part of their lives.

■ providing time for students to explore their thoughts and feelings in a reading log or journal. (Review "Keeping a Reading Log" [257-258] in *Writers INC* for an explanation of this activity and for a list of questions that will help students write about their reading. "More Than Mere Words" [259] offers additional reacting-to-reading ideas.)

- responding to their log entries. This is especially important if students need something clarified during their reading. Responses don't have to be detailed; simply show them with sincere comments that you are interested in their thoughts and feelings. (Refer to Nancie Atwell's *In the Middle* for suggestions for responding to students' logs.)

- providing time for students to share their thoughts and feelings with their classmates in group or class discussions. They might raise questions about their reading during a discussion, or they might share favorite or interesting journal entries.

"Once a person has seen his responses in action in a general way and how they are constantly functioning, literature becomes less a subject he learns in school than a special opportunity to engage the emotions and thoughts foremost in his mind."
— David Bleich

- allowing students a choice in their reading material. Students should have opportunities to read popular or classic titles of their own choosing. This means you should have a classroom library well stocked with popular and classic titles for young adults. (If you are interested in developing a classroom library, see our catalog for classroom sets of popular and classic titles arranged according to grade and interest level.)

Special Note: Don't worry. You won't have to abandon all of your favorite literature units if you make your program more student directed. You will, however, want to cut back on the amount of material you present to your students, and you will want to present it after your students have had a chance to explore their own thoughts and feelings about their reading.

What's the end result of such an approach?

Once students become more active participants, their attitude toward reading and literature will change. They will . . .

- read more willingly and more often.

- become more interested in the printed word in general, including their own writing.

- become more receptive to enrichment activities related to their reading.

- discover that they can think and write in a meaningful way about their reading.

- discover that literature can move them and enrich their lives.

Keeping a Reading-Response Journal

While students are "experiencing" a book, they should be encouraged to record their journey in a journal. Set aside class time specifically for journal writing. Students can use the following ideas as starting points for their writing, but encourage them to explore whatever issues they feel are important.

Plot and Character

- Simply "free-write" about the book for 5-10 minutes each day.

- Write a description of the character you think is the main character after reading the first chapter.

- After reading several chapters (or about half the book), predict what you think will happen.

- Write a short summary of every chapter (or every 10-15 pages if the chapters are long).

- When you are about halfway through the book, list the characters and briefly tell how you feel about each one of them. Do this again when you have completed the book. Did your feelings change?

- What character do you feel closest to after the first chapter? After you're halfway through the book? Why? Is this the same character you feel closest to when the book ends?

- Keep a time line or "chronolog" of events as they happen.
- Write a dialogue between you and one of the characters. What would you ask this character? How would he/she respond?
- How does the main character interact with other people? Do you like the way he/she treats other people?

Setting and Theme

- Write a description, draw a picture, or create a map of the setting(s).
- If your book is set in a particular country or place, jot down sentences that give you an idea of what that place is like. If your book occurs at a particular time in history, can you gather information about that time from this book? If so, make a list of your findings. If your book takes place in a small town during World War II, write in your own words what living there at that time must have been like. Did they have radio? Television? Cars? What songs were popular?
- Ask yourself this question: "What is the author trying to tell me in this book?"
- Identify important words or phrases in the book. Explain why they are important.
- Paste into your journal any newspaper or magazine articles you find which relate to the book or its themes in any way. You might want to search for some critiques of this book in the library, make copies, and include them.

Personal Reaction

- Make a list of the many different ways you feel while you read. Uneasy? Fearful? Crushed? Restless? Worried? Hopeful? Annoyed? Peaceful? Free? Sympathetic? Your class or some groups might choose to make a list of all the feelings that seem to be experienced when reading books.
- Record what was happening in the book when you were having a particular feeling. ("I was angry when . . . .")
- Pinpoint where you were in the book when you became so involved you didn't want to quit reading.

- What memories is this book triggering in you? List these memories and choose one or more to describe in greater detail.
- What new thoughts or ideas come to you as you are reading this book? Keep a list.
- Record anything that seems really important to you while you are reading.

Style and Word Choice

- Copy those sentences, quotes, and passages that move you in some way.
- Make a list of words from the book that you would like to know and use in your own writing.
- What skill are you working on as a writer? Watch how the author of this book uses that skill. Are you learning to show instead of tell? Copy some sentences or passages which you feel are excellent examples of this skill. Are you learning to write dialogue? How does this author get into and out of dialogue? Copy a few samples for your use.

Final Note: Discuss with your classmates the different techniques you are using for keeping a response journal. Find out what they are using and what is working well for them. Brainstorm together for other techniques that you might try.

Writing About Literature

"Writing about Literature" in *Writers INC* contains a thorough discussion of the book review as well as two exemplary student models, one for a nonfiction title and one for a work of fiction. Also included here are guidelines for responding to literature in a reading log. Of special interest will be the "Sample Reading Log Questions" which students can use to initiate personal responses to any form of literature. A comprehensive glossary of literary terms addressing everything from allegory to understatement follows in the next chapter. Students will find this glossary extremely helpful when they discuss and analyze literature.

Using Drama in the Classroom

"Those who have no fire in themselves cannot warm others."

RATIONALE: *Why incorporate drama?*

■ It's a proven fact that when a student is given an opportunity to learn something using more than one sense, the material will be assimilated easier and remembered longer.

■ It's a motivation to know your work will be read by others; why not "motivate" your students' writing and learning with full-sense drama activities?

■ It's healthy to exercise the body, the intellect, and the emotions; can you think of a better way to exercise all three than in monitored dramatic situations?

■ It's true that creativity, an important ingredient of successful writing, can be heightened through drama exercises.

■ It's also unfortunately true that language arts is not always the favorite subject of every student. It is difficult to make this a physically active, hands-on subject. Adding physical movement to your language arts program through drama activities increases interest in this subject and results in greater involvement of reluctant students.

■ Drama is fun! What's wrong with having fun while you're learning?

■ It's rapport building; it will help build classroom trust, a feeling of *esprit de corps,* a sense of community.

■ It's an opportunity for your students to see a different side of their teacher—that is, if you choose to participate in some of the activities.

■ It's communication! Communication is the goal of drama. It's pure, powerful, and very properly placed in any language arts curriculum.

Dramatic activities are not meant to stop the flow of a lesson or a writing project. Rather, they are meant to enhance or heighten the final product. When and how you use a dramatic activity depends on the nature of the work at hand.

Encouragement for Those Who Might Say . . .

"But I've never had a drama class in my life! I don't know how to teach drama, and I don't want to look like a fool in front of my class!"

You're not teaching drama; you're providing a positive environment for developing communication skills. If the "D" word makes you nervous, don't use it! Use *communication* instead; you'll be just as accurate.

There is nothing more natural than drama. It was one of the earliest ritualistic forms of communication and of teaching. Early tribes, for example, passed on their history through pantomime.

Start small and as your confidence builds, try more complex or longer activities. Enjoy the learning, and don't be afraid to let the kids lead the way. You might be the teacher that brings out the student no one else could! Your class might be the one that the kids talk about for years after graduation because you dared to involve the complete person in your teaching of communication.

PARTICIPATION:

These drama exercises should not only be for the gifted or more outgoing students who will volunteer enthusiastically for the activities. It is important to make sure that all students realize that this is a mandatory part of the course—just as any writing segment is.

What has worked well for me is having students put their names on index cards. Shuffle the cards, and it becomes the luck of the draw who does the activity first. If time does not allow all students to participate in one day's work, they know their names will be called during the next drama activity. In this way, everyone will get an equal opportunity to participate.

You might even be daring and put your own name on a card. What an opportunity to interact with a student in a totally different dimension! Or, you might use small groups so the entire class is engaged in the activity at the same time.

"Never tell people how to do things. Tell them what to do and they will surprise you with their ingenuity."

Getting-Started Activities

"What are you doing?"

The trick of this activity is that the participants never do what they say they're doing. Two students make up a team. "A" could be pretending to brush his teeth when "B" asks, "What are you doing?" "A" could say "jumping rope"; then "B" must begin to jump rope. But when "A" asks him what he's doing, "B" might say that he is throwing horseshoes, and so on. You never say what you're doing, or do what you're saying. Each team has one minute to get as many exchanges as possible. Each team will need a scorekeeper, and someone must also keep track of the time. Once a game begins, there may be no repeats. This creativity-building activity has been a hit with students from the fifth grade up.

Pantomime Vocabulary Builder

The purpose of this activity is to build vocabulary and classification powers. Begin with a starter word such as *vehicle, emotion, clothing, machine, gesture, walk,* or *person,* and let the students brainstorm in two to four groups for synonyms for their word. Allow them to use a dictionary or thesaurus if necessary. Supply each group with a separate starter word and small pieces of paper on which to write each synonym (a "type" of vehicle, emotion, clothing, etc.). Then, in turn, each group shows one piece of paper to the teacher and pantomimes the word written on it. Perhaps the word is *strut,* a synonym for *walk.* (The teacher must announce what the starter word is.) The other groups each have a spokesperson to whom the members give their ideas. In turn, each group's spokesperson guesses the type of walk. If it is correct, that team gets a point. If it is not, another group has an opportunity to guess. If no group guesses correctly, the teacher may award the point to the presenting group, if the synonym was accurately presented, or give no point and tell the word. The second group now begins the process. Other starter words include *country, state, president, food, furniture, occupation, sports, dances, nouns, verbs, adjectives,* and *adverbs.*

What if?

Have a student pantomime walking from one side of your room to the other, pretending that there is a violent rainstorm. Have the next student walk in a "storm" of goldfish, M & Ms, knives, money, babies, and so on. (Remember that it's been raining for hours so the ground is deep in whatever it has been raining.)

OR . . .

Have a student pantomime walking through a field of mud three feet deep. The next student may walk through a field of tightly penned chickens, a field of mine traps, a field of sleeping alligators, knee-deep water, etc.

Then, have the students write about why it was raining goldfish or something other than water, or have them write about why they were crossing a field of sleeping alligators, etc. Ask them to describe how it felt externally and internally, remembering as many details as possible from their pantomime. It might be helpful to explain this writing project to the class before the pantomime, so they will pay closer attention to how they feel while experiencing their "walk."

Reeling It In

Divide the class into five groups for this pantomime activity. When the first group is in front of the class, the teacher should announce a sense—sight, for example—and each member of the class should suggest something for the group to "see in their mind's eye" and react to as honestly as they can. It will be interesting to note that not all the students will react the same way to a suggested sight. Encourage creativity, but also honesty. Repeat with another group and another sense.

Building Vocabulary

What do we know about vocabulary development?

For one thing, we know there is a strong connection between a student's vocabulary and his or her reading ability. The same is true for a student's ability to listen, speak, and write. In fact, we now recognize that each person actually has four vocabularies, one each for reading, listening, speaking, and writing (listed here from largest to smallest). Although there is much overlap, students will always be able to recognize more words than they can produce. This is important to keep in mind as you develop a program of vocabulary development for your students.

Vocabulary development must also occur across the curriculum. Students must read, hear, speak, and write with the words they are attempting to learn in their classes. Anything less and the words will not become part of their permanent "producing" vocabulary.

Existing studies tell us two things: 1) giving students lists of vocabulary words with little or no context is not an efficient way to teach vocabulary; 2) students must be actively involved with the words they are attempting to learn.

Vocabulary-Building Strategies

The vocabulary-building strategies which follow have taken all of these points into consideration:

■ Previewing in Context

1. Select 5-6 words from a chapter or selection students are about to read.
2. Have students open their books to the page and paragraph in which each word is located. Ask them to find the word, read it in context, and try to figure out the meaning.
3. Have each student write down what they think each word means.
4. Discuss possible meanings and arrive at the correct definition in this context.

■ Self-Collection

1. Students should set aside a portion of their journals or notebooks to collect personal vocabulary.
2. Students can collect new and interesting words from any source, preferably outside of school.
3. Each journal entry should contain the word and the context in which it was used.
4. The student can then analyze the word using its context, word parts, and dictionary definitions.

■ Prefix, Suffix, Root Study

1. Students should learn the most common prefixes, suffixes, and roots.
2. For a complete study of the prefixes, suffixes, and roots used in our language, students can be assigned 3-4 word parts each week for the entire year (see lists for each level on pp. 64-65 of this booklet).
3. Students can be given a number of strategies for learning these word parts:

   ❏ Assign students one word part a day (every day except Monday, perhaps). As you are taking roll, students can write out the word part, the definition, a sample word, and a sentence using this word, which can then be exchanged and corrected.

   ❏ Students can then be asked to brainstorm for word associations or familiar words which will help them remember the meaning of each word part.

   ❏ Students can be challenged to combine the word parts they have studied into as many words as possible (perhaps in 5 minutes time, or as a challenge assignment for the next day). Special cards can also be used for this purpose.

Word Card	de re in	flex flect	ion or ible

- Students can also be challenged to create "new" words using the word parts they have learned. To qualify, a new word should be one that makes sense and might actually be used if it were known to a large number of people.
- Students can be asked to share their "new" word and challenge other students to guess what it means and to write a sentence (or two or three) in which they use this word.
- Students can start a special section in their notebooks for word parts they come across in newspapers, magazines, and their other classes.

■ **Context Clues Study**

1. Students should read and discuss the context clues section of their *Writers INC* handbook.
2. Students should practice identifying the types of context clues as they use the previewing and self-collection techniques.

■ **Other Forms of Word Study**

1. **Special groups.** Students can be introduced to special groups of words found in computer language, music, politics, advertising, etc.
2. **Word play.** A certain amount of "word play" is essential to growth in vocabulary. Any type of word game will work so long as it is appropriate for the level of the students.
3. **Word-A-Day.** At the beginning of the class period, a word is printed on the board (a word that a student can use in his reading, listening, writing, and speaking vocabularies). As students enter the classroom, they immediately grab a dictionary and look up the word. As a class, students discuss the meaning and agree on a definition and a part of speech. They then use the word in a sentence, showing that they know what the word means and how to use it correctly.

Each student jots this information into a notebook. Each page is divided by a line drawn vertically at a point about one third of the width of the page. On the left side of this line, the word is written. On the right side of the line, the part of speech, definition, and sentence are written. This allows the student to cover the definitions by simply folding the paper.

A written quiz can be given each Friday, covering the five words from the recent week and five words from any past weeks. The student must write the word in a sentence, proving again that he knows what the word means and how to use it.

Word Parts Study List

The following lists of word parts can be used as the basis of a vocabulary program for levels 9, 10, and 11.

LEVEL 9

Prefixes: anti (ant), bi (bis, bin), circum (circ), deca, di, ex (e, ec, ef), hemi (demi, semi), hex, il (ir, in, im), in (il, im), intro, mono, multi, non, penta, post, pre, quad, quint, re, self, sub, super (supr), tri, un, uni

Suffixes: able (ible), an (ian), ar (er, or), cide, cule (ling), en, ese, ess, ful, ion (sion, tion), ist, ity (ty), ize, less, ology, ward

Roots: anni (annu, enni), aster (astr), aud (aus), auto (aut), bibl, bio, breve, chrom, chron, cide, cise, cit, clud (clus, claus), corp, crat, cred, cycl (cyclo), dem, dent (dont), derm, dic (dict), domin, dorm, duc (duct), erg, fin, fix, flex (flect), form, fort (forc), fract (frag), geo, graph (gram), here (hes), hydr (hydro, hydra), ject, join (junct), jur (jus), juven, laut (lac, lot, lut), lic (licit), magn, mand, mania, meter, micro, migra, multi (multus), number (numer), omni, ortho, ped (pod), phon, pop, port, prehend, punct, reg (recti), rupt, sci, scrib (script), serv, spec (spect, spic), sphere, tele, tempo, terra, therm, tract (tra), typ, uni, vid (vis), zo

LEVEL 10

Prefixes: ambi (amb), amphi, bene (bon), by, co (con, col, cor, com), contra (counter), dia, dis (dif), eu (ev), extra (extro), fore, homo, inter, mis, ob (of, op, oc), para, per, peri, poly, pro, se, syn (sym, sys, syl), trans (tra), ultra, under, vice

Suffixes: ance (ancy), ate, cian, ish, ism, ive, ly, ment, ness, some, tude

Roots: ag (agi, ig, act), anthrop, arch, aug (auc), cap (cip, cept), capit (capt), carn, cause (cuse, cus), civ, clam (claim), cord (cor, card), cosm, crea, cresc (cret, crease, cru), dura, dynam, equi, fac (fact, fic, fect), leg, lit (liter), log (logo, ology), luc (lum, lus, lun), man, mar (mari, mer), medi, mega, mem, mit (miss), mob (mot, mov), mon, mori (mort, mors), nov, onym, oper, pac, pan, pater (patr), path (pathy), pend (pens, pond), phil, photo, plu (plur, plus), poli, portion, prim (prime), psych, put, salv (salu), sat (satis), scope, sen, sent (sens), sign (signi), sist (sta, stit, stet), solus, solv (solu), spir, spond (spons), string (strict), stru (struct), tact (tang, tag, tig, ting), test, tort (tors), vac, vert (vers), vict (vinc), voc

LEVEL 11

Prefixes: a (an), ab (abs, a), acro, ante, be, cata, cerebro, de, dys, epi, hyper, hypo, infra, intra, macro, mal, meta, miso, neo, oct, paleo, pseudo, retro, sex (sest)

Suffixes: asis (esis, osis), cy, dom, ee, ence (ency), et (ette), ice, ile, ine, ite, oid

Roots: acer (acid, acri), acu, ali (allo, alter), altus, am (amor), belli, calor, caus (caut), cognosc (gnosi), crit, cur (curs), cura, doc, don, dox, end (endo), fall (fals), fila (fili), flu (fluc, fluv), fum, gastro, germ, gloss (glot), glu (glo), greg, helio, hema (hemo), hetero, homo, ignis, later, levis, lith, liver (liber), loc (loco), loqu (locut), lude, matri (matro, matric), monstr (mist), morph, nasc (nat), neur, nom, nomen (nomin), nounce (nunci), nox (noc), pedo, pel (puls), phobia, plac (plais), plenus, pneuma (pneumon), pon (pos, pound), posse (potent), proto, que (qui), quies, ri (ridi, risi), rog (roga), sacr (sanc, secr), sangui, sed (sess, sid), sequ (secu, sue), simil (simul), somnus, soph, sume (sump), ten (tin, tain), tend (tent, tens), tom, tox, trib, tui (tuit, tut), turbo, vale (vali, valu), ven (vent), viv (vita, vivi), vol, volcan (vulcan), vor

Addressing Spelling

A recent nationwide study of 20,000 student essays at the college level revealed that spelling errors occurred more frequently than any other error by a factor of 300 percent. In *Writing: Children & Teachers at Work* (Heinemann, 1983), Donald Graves cites a survey given to parents that ranks spelling just below reading and math as a priority in instruction. Graves adds that writing placed eighth in the survey—which suggest that the public perceives that "spelling is more important than what it is for . . . writing." What do these findings indicate? Teachers at all levels must address spelling in some shape or form. Students not only need and deserve help with this skill, but the public demands it.

Direct Spelling Practices That Work

- Devoting approximately 10 minutes per day (two or three days a week) to direct instruction
- Presenting and studying words in short lists (8-10 words)
- Drawing words primarily from one of the many master lists citing words frequently used by student and adult writers (See 714 in *Writers INC.*)
- Studying the complete word rather than word parts or syllables
- Employing the pretest-study-test method of instruction
- Asking students to correct their own pretests
- Providing students with a strategy to learn how to spell new words (*Examine, pronounce, cover,* and *write*—repeated two or three times if needed—is one such strategy.)
- Linking spelling instruction, whenever possible, to the students' own writing

Spelling Practices to Avoid

- Isolating and studying the difficult parts in words
- Writing words over and over to learn them
- Examining spelling words in context
- Using spelling words in fill-in-the-blank exercises, prescribed writing scenarios, and so on
- Spending too much time on oral spelling exercises
- Focusing on spelling rules—which, generally speaking, does more harm than good
- Asking students to spell words they have difficulty reading

Writing and Learning Across the Curriculum

Active Learning in Action

Picture this:

An English classroom with too many students (33) and one teacher. There are no neat rows of desks and there is a hum of human voices. The walls and the blackboards are almost entirely covered with assorted posters and papers, and there are even a few pieces of advice on the ceiling. One states: "Show Your Potential." You have to look up to see it and that is the whole point. Your student guide tells you this. You are visiting this active-learning classroom, and you are wary of this student guide.

A student guide leads you to a group of four students in the far northeast corner of the room. These students introduce themselves. (They even stand and put out a hand—one of the interactive behaviors they have elected to adopt.) They tell you they are analyzing the précis their classmates have written about favorite books they read. They will use these to develop and "publish" a summer reading list for each member of the class. The school has given them enough paper to print 100 additional copies for distribution in the library. One student remarks that if they had had a little more time before school was out, they would have tried to obtain funds to publish lists for every student and for the public library.

Poetic Debate

Your guide moves you on to another group. These learners are sharing letters they wrote to Emily Dickinson. All the letters begin, "Emily, let me tell you who I am." This group is comprised of students who feel Emily Dickinson was the most boring poet who ever lived. They tell you that in the group working next to them, all the members "love" Emily. Starting tomorrow two members from each group will exchange places. The anti-Emily group is very excited about a piece they found in the latest issue of *The English Journal* . . . .

Wait. *The English Journal?* How do these kids know about *The English Journal?* "Our teacher lets us use them so we can design projects and get ideas. We use *Challenge* magazine, too, and some ideas books."

The next group you encounter is doing somewhat the same thing as the Emily Dickinson groups. They are constructing a poem which begins, "I sing myself." They have already written letters to "Walt," as they put it, and now are trying to emulate him. This is the last day they can work on their poems. "We have to have a rough draft of a piece about which author we'd most like to meet and where we would take him or her. That group over there got the idea because they found a piece in *The English Journal* about a humorist who would take Emily for a ride through the United States, and buy her sunglasses and have her eat sweet crunchy fried fish at the Booga Bottom Store."

A Correspondence Course

About this time you notice a man in a suit and tie sitting in a desk in the back corner. He is partially hidden by the three file cabinets along that wall. Sitting in a desk facing him is a student. They are studying a letter the student wrote to Midnight Oil (the Australian rock band).

"We all wrote letters this year. Lots of letters. We all got responses, too. See? That part of that wall is full of the letters we got back from people we wrote to. Our teacher has one up there from the queen of England . . . well, not really. It's from one of her ladies-in-waiting, but we like to say it's from the queen. Our teacher will be going to England in June, and she was hoping the queen would be making some public appearances so she might catch a glimpse of her. But the queen will be vacationing at Balmoral."

You would like to see who else has a letter on "The Writing Wall," but it's time to meet the teacher in the classroom. You start toward the man in the suit only to find your guide is approaching the group of people huddled together in the opposite corner of the room.

You see a smiling lady in this group. Your guide explains, "This is our teacher. That is Mr. Fields, the superintendent of schools. He is an excellent letter writer, so we asked him if he could give us some tips and advice. All those students signed up for an individual conference with him. He points to a list of names on the blackboard. He's only got about halfway down the list, so we won't talk to him. The students would be mad if we took their time."

> *"An education isn't how much you have committed to memory, or even how much you know. It's being able to differentiate between what you do know and what you don't."*
> — Anatole France

Literary Review

What is the teacher doing in the corner with this group of students? You're told this group wants to be certain to know every important literary term. They have memorized them and periodically test each other. Now they are in the final stages of putting together a booklet for each other containing definitions of the terms, an example from literature, and, if possible, an original example. "It has been a very long process," the teacher says. "These six students are left from eleven that started, but the ones who dropped out will probably complete their booklets next year. They are concerned they won't have the background knowledge they need for college.

Next, they are going to design a process they can use to continue their study of literature this summer and thereafter. I shouldn't be speaking for the students. I still forget that this is their classroom." She looks at each student and says, "They can speak for themselves."

Why would a teacher do this? Why go to all this trouble? Slowly it comes to you. Every student in that room was actively engaged in learning, actively engaged in finding out things for themselves. They were sources of information. Cutups? Class clowns? Bored individuals? They weren't anywhere in sight.

What can you do to promote active learning in your classroom? There are any number of active-learning approaches that you can work rather easily into any classroom. Each one of them requires that you modify your teaching to make it more student directed. A classroom like the one described above would take a great deal of time and planning to implement because it is such a departure from the typical classroom setting. But aim for it if you like it. Otherwise, do what you can today to make leaning more active in your classroom.

Approaches to Active Learning

Each one of the following approaches can be used with *Writers INC* to promote active learning.

- **Writing to Learn** (See pp. 70-75 in this booklet and topics 469-474 in *Writers INC*.)
- **Minilessons** (See pp. 93-127 in this teacher's guide.)
- **Firsthand Research** (See "Personalized Research," topics 138-139 in *Writers INC*.)
- **Problem Solving** (See "Thinking Clearly," topics 537-539.)
- **Open-Ended Questions** (See "Sample Reading Log Questions," topic 258.)
- **Cooperative Learning** (See topics 465-468 in *Writers INC*.)

Characteristics of Active and Passive Learning

Passive Learning . . .

- Students usually sit quietly and listen.
- Students use a text for nearly all "learning."
- The text is THE source of information.
- Nearly all questions require *right* answers.
- Activities require mainly lower-level thinking skills.
- Personal or imaginative thinking is seldom required.
- How-to-learn strategies never develop.
- Students don't grow as independent learners.

Active Learning . . .

- Students are actively involved in learning.
- Students use original sources and firsthand experiences in addition to texts.
- Students become sources of information.
- Students freely offer ideas, attitudes, and beliefs.
- Variation in answers is expected.
- An appreciation to learn and a desire to acquire and apply knowledge is fostered.
- Sudents develop how-to-learn strategies that will serve them for a lifetime.
- The students' self-esteem is enhanced.

Writing to Learn . . . Using Language (and *Writers INC*) Across the Curriculum

Q. What exactly is "writing to learn"?

A. Writing to learn is a method of learning which helps students get more out of their course material. It is thinking on paper—thinking to discover connections, describe processes, express emerging understandings, raise questions, and find answers. It is a method which students can use in all subjects at all ages.

Q. What is the purpose of writing to learn?

A. The main purpose is better thinking and learning. (Better writing is a by-product.) This is why writing to learn is not just for English teachers.

Q. What makes writing to learn work?

A. Writing is uniquely suited to foster abstract thinking. The linearity of writing—one word after another—leads to more coherent and sustained thought than simply thinking or speaking. Also, when writing is used, all students can respond, including those who are reluctant to answer out loud.

Q. What are the advantages of writing to learn for students?

A. Writing to learn provides students with a way of learning, not just a set of facts. It forces students to personalize—to internalize—learning so that they understand better and remember longer. It also encourages higher-level thinking skills.

Q. What are the advantages for teachers?

A. Teachers using writing to learn will see learning, thinking, and writing improve among their students. They will also notice improved communication, rapport, and motivation as students become more independent and more actively involved in the learning process. Also, teachers will come to rely less and less on "writing to show learning" which needs to be graded.

Q. How do you go about beginning a writing-to-learn program?

A. First of all, there is no one "program" for writing to learn. Teachers can begin with the chapter "Writing to Learn" in the *Writers INC* handbook. After reading, writing, and discussing your way through this chapter, both students and teachers should have a good idea of what writing to learn is all about.

Then the teacher must select from the wide variety of activities available those which best suit their needs and the needs of their students. Once an activity is selected, it is very important that students understand they are "writing to learn," not "writing to show learning." If they understand that they are not writing simply to please their teacher, but to personalize and better understand information, you are on your way.

Q. What kinds of topics are good for writing to learn?

A. Any topic that is worth knowing or thinking about is a good writing-to-learn topic. Teachers in subject areas where writing does not usually occur need only identify the "language components" in their subjects and select a writing activity which will work within the context and setting of the course.

Q. Is an essay test or research paper a good example of writing to learn?

A. No, these are examples of writing to show learning. The difference is that writing to learn focuses on the process of learning—thinking—rather than on the product of learning—factual information. "Writing to learn" often ends with unfinished writing; "writing to show learning" is usually a finished, graded product.

Q. What kind of writing is considered writing to learn?

A. Journal writing, learning logs, list making, recording observations, surveys, and any other writing activity which helps students personalize and make meaning out of what they are attempting to learn are all writing-to-learn activities.

Q. What does a teacher have to know before using writing to learn in the classroom?

A. Very little. The information in this booklet will give you more than enough information and ideas to get you started. Remember, too, that there is no "right way" to use writing to learn; it is up to the instructor to select from the wide range of activities those which are best suited to meet students' needs and accomplish course goals.

Q. Are there any highly recommended activities that can be used immediately?

A. Yes, learning logs, stop 'n write, and admit slips (or exit slips) are excellent activities to start with.

Q. What other materials would be helpful in setting up a writing-to-learn program?

A. You can refer to any of the resources listed below (which were used in compiling the information in this packet). Titles are Heinemann/Boynton-Cook publications unless otherwise noted.

Recommended Reading:

A Community of Writers — Steven Zemelman and Harvey Daniels

Learning to Write / Writing to Learn — John S. Mayher, Nancy Lester, Gordon M. Pradl

Roots in the Sawdust: Writing to Learn across the Disciplines — Anne Ruggles Gere, ed. (Available through NCTE)

Writing to Learn: 10 Things You Should Know

Writers INC contains a special section on "Writing to Learn." Students are given the background necessary to begin using *writing* to learn, especially in journals and learning logs. The following information provides both teacher and student with additional writing-to-learn ideas.

1 **Writing to learn may be the best way we know to achieve the overall goal of education:** providing students with an effective way of thinking and learning.

2 **Writing to learn is a method of learning which helps students get more out of their material.** It enables teachers and students to focus on the process of learning—thinking—rather than the product of learning—factual information. (In the process, factual information is learned.)

3 **Writing to learn is student centered.** The ideas and motivation for writing come mainly from the students who are quick to realize that writing can lead to more effective learning (and better grades).

4 **Writing to learn enables students to personalize/internalize learning** so that they can better understand and remember.

5 **Writing to learn encourages abstract, higher-level thinking.** The linearity of writing—one word after the other—leads to more coherent and sustained thought than mere thinking or speaking.

6 **Writing-to-learn activities differ from traditional writing activities** in several important ways:

WRITING TO LEARN	Formal writing
SPONTANEOUS	planned
SHORT	lengthy
EXPLORATORY	authoritative
EXPRESSIVE	transactional
INFORMAL	formal
PERSONAL	impersonal
(student centered)	(teacher centered)
UNEDITED/UNFINISHED	polished
UNGRADED	graded

7 **Writing to learn is not the same as writing to show learning.** Its purpose is learning, not showing what has already been learned. Writing to learn should be thought of as a tool for learning, a tool that works best when it is comfortable in the hands of the user. Students should use the language they "think" in—language which is personal, informal, colloquial—as close to their everyday speech as possible. Compare the two samples below in which the teacher had asked each student to write a short paragraph in response to a reading assignment. The paragraphs were to show, in the students' own words, their reactions to the material as well as what they had learned. Otto, reacting to a section on diffusion, wrote this:

> Substances leave and enter the cells by diffusion and osmosis. Diffusion is when molecules move from an area of greater concentration to an area of less concentration. Concentration is the amount of material per a unit volume. The more molecules, the greater concentration. Diffusion only occurs when a substance is in a solution. In order for sugar and starch and protein to leave the cells, they must break apart into substances that can dissolve in body fluids. Molecules can move through the membrane by diffusion. Osmosis is the diffusion of water through a membrane. Food and oxygen diffuse from the blood through the cell membrane and into the blood.

Virtually all of the language here is that of the text; it offers none of Otto's personal reactions nor makes any connections with his life. Otto will most likely forget what he has written within a relatively short time. In contrast, Emily wrote this:

> In reading this section I thought of the lab that I did on diffusion. I knew something about diffusion, but I didn't know it. I thought of how neat it was that these molecules seemed to have a brain. It's like they knew and have always known what to do. How to diffuse.

Emily does not summarize or repeat the material but interprets and reacts to it by connecting it to previous experiences and giving her personal response. In doing so she opens up a new range of possible questions; for instance, what is the "brain" behind the process of diffusion?

Unfortunately, both Emily and Otto received identically uninformative feedback from their teacher: a check on the top of the paper. Not surprisingly, they both thought they had done an adequate job and continued to do the same kind of learning logs throughout the term. Once students have learned how to do this kind of assignment, as in Emily's case, a check may be an adequate teacher response; but while they are learning to do it, more informative feedback must be given. Students, like teachers, have learned to play the school game in the conventional repetition/fill-in-the-blank pattern; whether or not they like it, it is familiar and safe. Putting more responsibility on students to become active learners does work, but it requires careful attention to the process of transition.

8 **Writing to learn allows all teachers to be teachers of writing and thinking.** Writing is both an internal (content) and external (mechanics) activity. Since all teachers are experts in their content area, they are well equipped to help students with the internal side of writing. They can help students gather, organize, and react to the content of their writing. (By using their handbooks, students are able to do much of their own editing and proofreading.)

9 **Learning works best as a dialogue, not a monologue.** Writing to learn makes it possible for a teacher to carry on a dialogue with 25 students at once.

10 **There is no "right way" to use writing to learn.** Students should be introduced to a variety of activities that they can use writing-to-learn both in and out of the classroom. They should be allowed to experiment and to create writing-to-learn activities of their own. In fact, the only prerequisite is that the risk of grading must be eliminated; only then will uninhibited thinking and personalizing take place. The list on the following pages contains activities which can be used effectively in a variety of situations.

Writing-to-Learn Activities

The following activities can be used to promote writing to learn. Teachers (and students) should experiment with a variety of activities and then decide on two or three which would best suit a particular course.

Active note taking: Students are asked to divide a page in half. On the left side, they are to record notes from their reading, and on the right side, they are to write comments or questions about the material they have read. This written dialogue makes note taking much more meaningful and provides students with material for class discussion. Among the comments students can make are the following:

■ a **comment** on what memory or feeling a particular idea brings to mind,

■ a **reaction** to a particular point which they strongly agree or disagree with,

■ a **question** about a concept that confuses them,

■ a **paraphrase** of a difficult or complex idea,

■ a **discussion** of the importance or significance of the material,

■ or a **response** to an idea that confirms or questions a particular belief.

Admit slips: Admit slips are brief pieces of writing (usually fit on half sheets of paper) which can be collected as "admission" to class. The teacher can read several aloud (without naming the writer) to help students focus on the day's lesson. Admit slips can be a summary of last night's reading, questions about class material, requests for teachers to review a particular point, or anything else students may have on their minds.

Bio-poems: Bio-poems enable students to synthesize learning because they must select precise language to fit into this form. (*NOTE:* Even though the bio-poem is set up to describe "characters," it can also be used to describe complex terms or concepts such as *photosynthesis, inflation,* etc.) Bio-poems encourage metaphorical and other higher-level thinking. A bio-poem follows this pattern:

BIO-POEM

Line 1. First name

Line 2. Four traits that describe the character

Line 3. Relative ("brother," "sister," "daughter," etc.) of _____

Line 4. Lover of _____ (list three things or people)

Line 5. Who feels _____ (three items)

Line 6. Who needs _____ (three items)

Line 7. Who fears _____ (three items)

Line 8. Who gives _____ (three items)

Line 9. Who would like to see _____ (three items)

Line 10. Resident of _____

Line 11. Last name

Brainstorming: Brainstorming (*list storming*) is writing done for the purpose of collecting as many ideas as possible on a particular topic. Students will come away with a variety of approaches which might be used to further develop a writing or discussion topic. In brainstorming, everything is written down, even if it seems at the time to be a weak or somewhat irrelevant idea.

Class minutes: One student is selected each day to keep minutes of the class lesson (including questions and comments) to be written up for the following class. That student can either read or distribute copies of the minutes at the start of the next class. Reading and correcting these minutes can serve as an excellent review, as well as a good listening exercise.

Clustering: Clustering is a special form of writing to learn which begins by placing a key word (nucleus word) in the center of the page. For example, suppose students were to write a paper on "responsibility" and what it means to them. *Responsibility* or *duty* would be an obvious nucleus word. Students would then record words which come to mind when they think of this word. They should record every word, circle it, and draw a line connecting it to the closest related word.

Completions: By completing an open-ended sentence (which the teacher or other students provide) in as many ways as possible, students are pushed to look at a subject in many different ways. Writing completions also helps students focus their thinking on a particular lesson or concept.

Correspondence: One of the most valuable benefits of writing to learn is that it provides many opportunities for students to communicate with their teachers, often in a sincere, anonymous way. If no writing-to-learn activity seems to bring about this kind of open communication, teachers should set up a channel (suggestion box, mailbox, special reply notes, etc.) which encourages students to communicate freely and honestly.

Creative definitions: As in the game "Fictionary," students are asked to write out definitions for new words. Other students are then asked to figure out whether the definition is fact or fiction. When students are given the actual definition, there is a much better chance they will remember it.

Dialogues: Students create an imaginary dialogue between themselves and a character (a public or historical figure, for example) or between two characters. The dialogue will bring to life much of the information being studied about the life or times of the subject.

Dramatic scenarios: Writers are projected into a unit of study and asked to develop a scenario (plot) which can be played out in writing. If the unit is World War II, for example, students might put themselves in President Truman's shoes the day before he decided to drop the atomic bomb on Hiroshima, and create a scenario of what they think this dramatic time in history may have been like.

Exit slips: Students are asked to write a short piece at the end of class in which they summarize, evaluate, or question something about the day's lesson. Students must turn in their exit slips in order to leave the classroom. Teachers can use the exit slips as a way of assessing the success of the lesson and deciding what needs to be reviewed before going on with the next lesson.

Fact/values lists: When a new topic is being introduced, students write down everything they know to be a fact on the left side of their papers, and everything they "believe, feel, or suspect" about the topic on the right. Students will not only become immediately involved with the new topic, but sharing these lists is bound to provide some interesting introductory material for the whole class.

First thoughts: Students write or list their immediate impressions (or what they already know) about a topic they are preparing to study. These writings will help students focus on the task at hand and will also serve as a point of reference to measure learning.

Focused writings: Writers are asked to concentrate on a single topic (or one particular aspect of a topic) and write nonstop for a certain amount of time. Like brainstorming, focused writing allows students to see how much (or how little) they have to say on a particular topic.

Free writing: Students write nonstop on a particular subject for a certain amount of time. During a free writing, students often discover things about a particular subject they weren't aware they knew. They often discover connections or personal associations which were not at first obvious. (See "Guidelines for Free Writing" in *Writers INC*.)

How-to writing: Students are asked to write instructions or directions on how to perform a certain task. This will help students both clarify and remember. Ideally, students would then be able to test their writing on someone who does not already know how the task is performed.

Instant versions: Students are given a composition assignment about a certain subject and then asked to pretend they are actually composing a final draft long before they are ready. Writing instant versions can help students clarify ideas and focus on "the big picture," as well as discover how much they know (or don't know) about the subject being studied.

Journals: Journals are places for students to keep their personal writings, including any of the writing-to-learn activities in this list. Often called "learning logs," journals allow students to record their impressions, questions, comments, discoveries, etc. about any subject, including the positive review given below by a student. (See "Guidelines for Journal Writing" in *Writers INC*.)

"This journal has got to be the best thing that's hit this chemistry class. For once the teacher has direct communication with every member of the class. . . . Thank you very much for all the help this journal has been to me."

Key word: Students can be asked to write on a key word or concept connected to the lesson. By doing a focused writing in which they attempt to "define" a key word or "summarize" a concept, students are given an opportunity to consolidate and internalize the information being presented.

Learning logs: A learning log is a journal (notebook) in which students keep their notes, thoughts, and personal reactions to the subject. (See "Guidelines to Keeping a Learning Log" in *Writers INC*; also see "Personal Writing Books" in your Write Source catalog.)

Listing: Freely listing ideas as they come to mind is another effective writing-to-learn activity. Students can begin with any idea related to the subject and simply list all the thoughts and details which come to mind. Listing can be very useful as a quick review or progress check.

Metacognition: Students are asked to write about their own thinking process, including where in the process they understood (or got lost) for the first time and how they went on from there. "Thinking about thinking" is especially useful in math and science.

Observation reports: The classic observation report has long been a staple in science labs. The objective is to collect data from close observation of objects, processes, and events. It is important to remember, however, that as with any writing-to-learn activity, an observation report should be written in language which allows students to personalize or internalize the information being written about.

Predicting: Students are stopped at a key point in a lesson and asked to write what they think will happen next. This works especially well with lessons which have a strong cause and effect relationship.

Question of the day: Writers are asked to respond to a question (often a "What if . . . ?" or "Why?") which is important to a clear understanding of the lesson or which prompts students to think beyond the obvious.

Stop 'n Write: At any point in a class discussion, students can be asked to stop and write. This will allow students a chance to evaluate their understanding of the topic, to reflect on what has been said, and to question anything which may be bothering them. These writings also help teachers assess how the lesson is progressing. (See "Predicting," above.)

Student teachers: An excellent way to encourage students to personalize or internalize class material is to have them construct their own mathematics word problems, science experiments, and discussion questions (which can be used for reviewing or testing). This is a great way to replace routine end-of-the-chapter or workbook questions with questions which students actually wonder about or feel are worth answering.

Summing up: Students are asked to sum up what was covered in a particular lesson by writing about its importance, a possible result, a next step, or a general impression left with them.

Unsent letters: Letters can be written to any person on any topic related to the subject being studied. Unsent letters allow students to become personally involved with the subject matter and enable them to write about what they know (or don't know) to someone else, imagined or real.

Warm-ups: Students can be asked to write for the first 5 or 10 minutes of class. The writing can be a question of the day, a free writing, a focused writing, or any other writing-to-learn activity which is appropriate. Warm-ups not only help students focus on the lesson at hand, but also give them a routine which helps break social contact at the beginning of each class.

Writing groups: Students can benefit greatly from working in groups. The writing which comes from a group discussion or brainstorming session can be either an individual or a collaborative effort. Group response to the writing can help students further clarify their thinking and writing. Group writing works especially well for quick summaries or short observation reports. (See "Group Advising and Revising" in *Writers INC*.)

See Writers File for additional information on "Writing Across the Curriculum."

Thinking to Learn

"Believe all students can think, not just the gifted ones. Let your students know that thinking is a goal. Create the right climate and model it."
— Arthur L. Costa

The market for teaching thinking was bullish at the end of the '80s, with articles regularly appearing in *Educational Leadership,* NCTE publications, and numerous other influential collections. Outstanding proponents of broader and better integrated approaches to thinking—leaders such as David Perkins, Art Costa, Richard Paul, Robin Fogarty, Barry Beyer, and others—were writing and speaking and inspiring teachers all over the country to "rethink" their classrooms.

Teacher Reaction

Many teachers have read and listened to what the experts have to say and, to some degree, have made thinking an important part of their curriculum.

Other teachers know that they should be challenging their students to think more critically and creatively, but they're not sure how to go about it. They wonder, in fact, if thinking is a skill which can be taught. Their concern is justified. Some educators say that effective thinking is a disposition or a temperament rather than a skill. Teachers are used to teaching skills, but teaching a disposition is another matter.

Then, of course, there are those teachers who wonder why so much fuss is being made about thinking. They say that their students have been thinking all along in their classrooms, and they're not about to change anything, thank you.

Creating a Thinking Climate in Your Classroom

For those of you who are ready to make your classrooms more "thinking oriented," we feel Arthur L. Costa offers the best advice in *Developing Minds* (ASCD, 1985). He suggests teachers teach **for thinking** (by creating the right classroom climate), **about thinking** (by helping students be more aware of their own think-

ing), and **of thinking** (by teaching thinking skills).

Teaching for Thinking

How can you create a thinking climate in your classroom? Read on and find out.

- Personalize the learning in your classroom. Students will approach learning more thoughtfully when the subject matter means something to them personally. Common sense (plus plenty of studies) tells us students won't become thoughtfully involved in work that is not relevant to them personally. What does this mean to you? Don't teach out of a textbook. Use the students' own thoughts, feelings, and interests as starting points for thinking and learning.

- Promote activities that have heretofore been considered fillers: stories, poems, posters, letters, parodies, riddles, debates, discussions, etc. These are the types of activities that get students *actively* thinking and learning. (Basic skills activity sheets generally do not promote thinking.)

- Engage your students in projects. Have them produce a class newspaper or magazine. Have them write and produce a play, a news show. Have them develop instructional manuals for skateboarding or car repair. There are any number of challenging thinking activities built into long-range projects.

- Promote collaborative learning. Collaboration is at the heart of learning outside of school. We learn how to ride, fish, bake, fix, etc., with the help of friends and family members. Collaborative learning gets people actively involved, gets them thinking, and gets them learning. It should be an important element in a thinking classroom. (See "Group Skills" in *Writers INC* and "Collaborative Learning" in this booklet for more information.)

 Hint Have your students work in writing groups. The give-and-take among students during writing projects promotes active thinking and better writing. (See "Group Advising and Revising" in *Writers INC* for guidelines.)

■ Promote open-ended, active learning in your classroom. Give your students every opportunity to explore, take risks, and make mistakes in your classroom. Ask them open-ended questions. Initiate role-playing activities, dramatic scenarios (see pp. 61-62 in this booklet), discussions, and debates. Pose problems, search for alternatives, test hypotheses, and, generally, challenge your students to think and act for themselves.

Hint Have students "Stop 'n Write" as well as write in a personal journal. There's no better way for them to explore their thoughts and feelings. (See "Journal Writing" in *Writers INC* for guidelines. Also see "Stop 'n Write" on p. 75 and "Keeping a Reading-Response Journal" on pp. 59-60 in this booklet.)

Teaching About Thinking

Experts believe it's important that teachers help students think about their own thinking (metacognition). Focusing on one's thinking process leads to better thinking and learning. Here are some things you can do to help students metacogitate:

■ Discuss with students how the brain works. Discuss left-brain thinking versus right-brain thinking. (See "Getting to Know Your Brain" in *Writers INC* for help.) Consider a discussion of artificial intelligence as well.

■ Select biographies of famous thinkers to share with your students.

■ Discuss with your students creative thinking, logical thinking, the connection between thinking and writing, the characteristics of effective thinkers, etc. (See the thinking section in *Writers INC* for help with this.)

■ Help students think about their own learning. Have them estimate how long an assignment will take. Have them determine what materials they will need to complete an assignment. Help them manage their work by breaking down challenging assignments into specific tasks. Help them find someone in class who can help them if they get stuck. Have them keep track of their progress during an extended project in a personal journal and so on.

■ Encourage students to take pride in their work. Remind them that their work is a reflection of their very own thinking. Have them evaluate their work upon its completion. They should consider what they liked or disliked about an assignment as well as what they succeeded at and what they need to work on. (See "Learning Logs" in *Writers INC* for more information.)

■ Remind students that it's all right to make mistakes, to get stuck, to reach dead ends. Give students an opportunity to talk or write about their thoughts and feelings when things aren't going well. Help them learn from these experiences.

■ Encourage students to connect what they have already learned to new information. Also, take every opportunity to connect what they are learning to their personal lives. If you want to discuss **evaluating**, why not have students evaluate the merits of one pair of popular jeans versus another, of one popular pizza versus another, of one way of volunteering their services versus another?

Teaching of Thinking

A third component in a thinking classroom includes direct instruction of thinking skills. Here's how to work thinking skills into your curriculum.

■ Review a taxonomy of thinking skills, and select a limited number to emphasize throughout the year—perhaps one comprehension skill (summarizing), one analyzing skill (classifying), one synthesizing skill (predicting), and one evaluating skill (persuading). (See page 247 in *Writers INC* for a list of thinking skills.)

■ Produce your own activities for instruction or use reputable thinking materials that are commercially produced.

■ Arthur Costa suggests that these skills should be not only worked into the general content area but taught independently in thinking activities. He suggests spending two or three hours per week in the direct teaching of thinking skills—until students have "mastered" these skills.

- Planning Thinking-Skills Lessons: A thinking-skill lesson plan should follow this general format:
  1. Introduce the skill. (Find out what the students already know about it.)
  2. Demonstrate the skill. (Get your students actively involved in your "demonstration.")
  3. Have your students apply this skill in an activity. (Give them an opportunity to work in pairs.)
  4. Follow up with a discussion of the activity. (That is, have students reflect on the thinking they have done.)
- Develop specific thinking activities which complement the "Thinking to Learn" section in *Writers INC*. You might
  - ❏ have students discuss the thinking process and "why do we think?" (See 525-526.)
  - ❏ have students refer to the section on "Getting to Know Your Brain" and prepare explanations (in small groups) of the structure and function of the brain, left brain/ right brain, thinking phases, etc. (See 528-531.)
  - ❏ have students refer to the "thinking operations" chart (542) regularly to get a visual sense of the kinds of thinking people do.
  - ❏ provide your students with a number of opportunities to focus on specific levels of thinking in writing assignments, essay tests, and projects.
  - ❏ give your students opportunities to think and write creatively. (See 532-536.)
  - ❏ give them opportunities to think and write (and speak) logically. (See 543-557.)

What's the end result of making thinking an important part of your curriculum? Your students will become more tuned in to learning because they will become better equipped to think and learn for themselves. They will become active learners and make your classroom an exciting and stimulating place to be. And they will challenge you and make you more excited about teaching.

Talking to Learn

"There is no hope of building a successful program in reading or writing on an inadequate base of oral language."
— Allen & Kellner

Many teachers have proven that talking to learn (verbalizing) is one of the most powerful ways for students to learn. These teachers have been designing and using a variety of effective ways for students to verbalize in classrooms because they know students will comprehend in a lasting way. Some of the activities teachers have been using are very basic; others are more complex.

Basic Talking-to-Learn Activities

On pages 79-80 in the collaborative learning section of this booklet, you will find three basic talking-to-learn strategies which are appropriate for any content area. After experimenting with these basic talking techniques, students will be better prepared for the following talking-to-learn activities in whole class or small group (four to five students) discussions:

■ Nerf Ball Discussion

Instead of merely calling on a student who raises his/her hand, toss a ball. When finished, that student can toss the ball to another student who has raised his hand or back to the teacher.

■ Talk-and-Yield Discussion

Use with either a whole class or small groups. The instructor picks the first speaker. When that speaker is finished, he/she picks the next speaker. There are no repeat speakers until everyone has had a turn, UNLESS the speaker who has not spoken volunteers to yield to a previous speaker who wants to make a point.

■ Read and Speak

Individual students read aloud a piece of writing which impresses them. This may be a page from a novel, a poem, a newspaper article, a scene from a short story or play. You may also have students read sentences or paragraphs from their own writing or another student's writing. After the reading the speaker explains why he thinks this piece is worthwhile, exciting, or well-done. Finally, he asks for questions from the class.

Using this method with textbooks can be especially effective. Students may choose the data in the text which most interested or surprised them, or they may introduce and read a portion from a piece of supplemental material that is germane to the topic. This could include current magazine and newspaper articles, novels, short stories, poems, letters, and even songs.

■ Talk-and-Record Sessions

(For evaluating group discussions)

When it is time for a discussion session, form groups of three to five students. Give each group a tape recorder, discussion guidelines and instructions, and plenty of time to develop their discussions. Upon completion of this group discussion, simply collect the recorded tapes, evaluate the work of each group, and during the next class period, share your observations with the class.

Why is talking to learn so powerful?

It is true that, at first, students will feel uncomfortable when vocalizing because they fear others will misinterpret what they say. It is also true that students at times will get lost in their own argument and lose their train of thought. However, these are not reasons to avoid or abandon talking to learn; rather they are the very reasons to provide students with many opportunities to talk. Talking to learn gives speakers AND listeners a chance to practice real-life speaking and thinking skills while they gather content data and information.

What can you do to make talking to learn work in your classroom?

1. Teach group skills. Require students to practice group skills when they work in groups.

2. Start with one of the basic talking-to-learn patterns. (You might use one of these patterns to introduce your students to the information about group skills.)

3. Schedule a formal conference with each group whenever a project is lengthy. In formal conferences you can model how talking together can be a productive process. Conferences are also a management tool. You will discover what the group is doing, who is contributing, who is practicing group skills, and what their needs are.

4. Make yourself available for informal sessions with small groups also.

Collaborative Learning

"Three men helping one another will do as much as six men singly."
– Spanish Proverb

Collaborative (cooperative) learning is a powerful classroom strategy for both teachers and students. Collaborative learning is working together as we have always tried to do, but with new knowledge about group dynamics, borrowed largely from the areas of communication and psychology.

Obviously, you already know a lot about cooperative learning. You have been or are a member of many groups—families, sport teams, community groups, faculty committees, and so forth.

Sometimes when we look at these groups, we tend to remember how ineffective they can be. It might be we feel we have a large body of knowledge about what NOT to do. This is okay. If nothing else, this is an incentive toward discovering what TO DO.

So what should a teacher who wants to use collaborative learning do?

First, we suggest that you experiment with collaborative learning before deciding if this classroom strategy is for you and your students. We provide three strategies you can use for this experimentation. The group skills you will want to work with are described in *Writers INC*.

While you are experimenting, keep these points in mind:

1. Collaborative learning allows teachers to move away from the front of the room and rely far less on lecturing.
2. Collaborative learning provides students with one of the most powerful ways to learn—verbalization.
3. Collaborative learning gives students more ownership of their learning and therefore motivates them to become better students.

Three Strategies That Work

The three strategies you can use for experimentation follow:

1. Tell/Retell Groups

Application: Any reading-to-learn activity

Recommended group size: 2 (3 in one group if you have an uneven number of students)

Group skills to emphasize: Listen actively, listen accurately, and offer words of encouragement.

STEP 1: One member reads a portion of the assigned material; the second member becomes an "active listener."

STEP 2: The second member tells what he/she heard; the first member becomes the "active listener." They decide *together* what the essential information is. (It's okay for them to look back at the reading material.)

STEP 3: Reverse roles and read the next portion.

2. Smart Groups

Application: Any reading-to-learn activity

Recommended group size: 2

Group skills to emphasize: Request help or clarification when needed, offer to explain or clarify, and never use put-downs.

STEP 1: Both students read assigned material. While reading, they put a faint check mark beside each paragraph they understand and a question mark beside any sentence, word, or paragraph they do not completely understand.

STEP 2: At each question mark, team members ask for help and clarification. If they both have questions, they try *together* to make sense of the material. If they both agree to seek outside help, they may consult another team or the teacher. If time allows, they may share what they remember about the passages they both understand.

3. Up-with-Your-Head Groups

Application: Checking comprehension and reviewing

Recommended group size: 4-5

Group skills to emphasize: Help a group reach a decision, learn how to disagree, and learn from disagreements.

STEP 1: Ask each student to number off within each group.

STEP 2: The teacher or a panel of students asks a question about the material that has been read.

STEP 3: Each group "puts their heads together" to make sure every member in their group knows an/the answer. When the question is an "open" question (one without a "correct" answer), the group reaches a consensus of opinion.

STEP 4: The questioner calls a number (1, 2, 3, 4, 5), and students with the corresponding number raise their hands to respond. When the question requires "an" answer, only one student need reply; but when the question is "open," a member from each group may reply.

What's the Next Step?

You will probably have many questions after experimenting. Questions such as these are common: "What is the teacher doing while students work?" "How do I assess student work?" "What happens when one group finishes before others?" "What is the best way to form groups?" "Are there more ways to use cooperative learning?"

We suggest that you order one of the many professional books available on collaborative learning. Many other sources of information also exist. Ask other teachers, your curriculum director, and your department head. Check with local colleges.

Daily Writing and Language Practice

Scavenger Hunts

The "scavenger hunts" on the following pages provide students with numerous opportunities for using the handbook. By becoming familiar with the contents and usage of the handbook, students will naturally use it more often as each need arises. Continued use will build confidence and help students become more self-reliant as editors and proofreaders of their own writing.

Implementation

There are many ways the scavenger hunts can be used in and out of the classroom. Probably the best way to begin is to simply read one of the scavenger hunts to your students at some point during class and observe them as they "hunt." You will undoubtedly have to help a number of your students, especially if they aren't in the habit of using an index. (The index is the key to using the student handbook since each topic is assigned its own "topic number"; these topic numbers—not page numbers—are listed in the index.)

Once a majority of students have found the correct information, you can ask them to share their answer and—just as importantly—where and how they found it. You might then try a second scavenger hunt to reinforce what has just been demonstrated.

After students get the hang of it, scavenger hunts can be used whenever they are needed—or whenever time permits. You might assign one at the end of the hour for the following day, especially if you plan to discuss that topic the following day. By directing students so specifically, you can help them focus on the important ideas in their reading—a valuable searching and reading strategy.

You can also ask students to make up scavenger hunts of their own—either because they found something very useful they would like to share or because they would like to "challenge" their classmates to find a rather obscure bit of information.

No matter how you use them, scavenger hunts can serve well as both a teaching and a learning strategy.

Level 9 Scavenger Hunts

Topic number 034
Page 28

Your teacher has told you to select a quotation as a writing topic for tomorrow. Where in your handbook will you find writing topics? Which quotation would you choose to write about?
   (Sample writing topics are found at topic number 034. Answers will vary.)

Topic number 053
Page 36

Your writing suffers from "primer style." What is this ailment and what's the cure?
   (Ailment: "Primer Style" is a style with many short, choppy sentences without effective connections. Cure: Do some careful sentence combining.)

Topic number 090
Page 45

You've been told to organize your essay into stronger paragraphs. What really are paragraphs anyway?
   (a series of related sentences which work together to develop a specific topic or idea)

Topic number 091 **Page 46**	*A friend is having trouble writing topic sentences. What formula does your handbook suggest that will help?* (your limited topic + a specific impression = a topic sentence)
Topic number 098 **Page 49**	*One of the most common ways to organize the details in your paragraphs is by time. What are the other ways?* (order of location, illustration, climax, cause and effect, comparison, definition)
Topic number 196 **Page 111**	*You need to find an article from* Sports Illustrated *on tennis stars of the 1980's. Where in the library do you look?* (*Readers' Guide to Periodical Literature*)
Topic number 201 **Page 115**	*In what way is a thesaurus the opposite of a dictionary?* (You go to a dictionary when you know the word and need the definition, a thesaurus when you know the definition and need the word.)
Topic number 202 **Page 116**	*In a dictionary, what part of speech is "v.i." an abbreviation for?* (intransitive verb)
Topic number 287 **Page 153** (OR: topic 073, page 42)	*So what if you've used a cliche? What's wrong with that?* (A cliche is an overused word or phrase which is not very effective.)
Topic number 308 **Page 154**	*You have to write an epigram. What are you going to be writing?* (a brief, witty poem or saying such as "There never was a good war or a bad peace." Ben Franklin)
Topic number 313 **Page 154**	*What is a "figure of speech," and which ones are most commonly used?* (a literary device used to create a special meaning through emotional and connotative use of words: personification, simile, metaphor)
Topic number 411 **Page 164**	*Let's say you're planning to write a business letter to ask about a summer job; where do you place your address on the letter?* (about an inch from the the top of the page)
Topic numbers **433-434** **Pages 180-181**	*If it's not a new sports car, what is the SQ3R?* (a method to help you remember what you read)
Topic number 443 **Page 185**	*When you are trying to improve your vocabulary skills, how do you use word parts to learn new words?* (By studying the structure of a single word [the prefix, root, and suffix which make up the word], it is possible to understand the meaning of that word.)

Topic number 444
Page 186

What are three sources from which you can "pick up" new words to improve your vocabulary?

(television, radio, conversation, music, commercials, magazines, mythology)

Topic number 475
Page 210

You have to take an essay test tomorrow. Which guidelines in Writers INC *will be most helpful?*

(Answers may vary: Listen carefully to instructions. Watch the time carefully. Read all the essay questions carefully.)

Topic number 620
Page 261

If you are combining short sentences into longer ones, when do you use a semicolon?

(to join independent clauses which are not connected with a coordinating conjunction)

Topic number 713
Page 278

You would like to become a better speller, but don't know how. What advice does Writers INC *offer?*

(Be patient, check the correct pronunciation, check the meaning and history . . .)

Topic number 942
Page 314

When avoiding sexism (as you should), what salutations are acceptable in a business letter?

(Dear Madam or Sir, Dear Personnel Officer, etc.)

Topic number 952
Page 317

A bunny is a young rabbit, and a pup is a young dog. What is a young elephant?

(calf)

Topic number 956
Page 320

Your birthday is December 19th. What sign of the zodiac is that?
(Sagittarius)

Topic number 961
Page 328

Seattle, Washington, is farther north than Toronto, Canada! What other United States cities are north of Toronto?
(Anchorage, Nome, Spokane, Duluth, etc.)

Topic number 963
Page 342

The 22nd Amendment to the Constitution limits the terms of the U.S. president. What year was it ratified?
(1951)

Topic number 966
Page 345

Who was Ulysses S. Grant's first vice president?
(Schuyler Colfax)

Topic number 967
Page 345

In the order of succession to the presidency of the United States, who is fourth in line?
(secretary of state)

Topic number 968
Page 346
(Page 348 in
1st Edition)

All good things must come to an end. What final computer command statement stops the program and returns the control to the user?

(END)

© Write Source, Box 460, Burlington, WI 53105

Level 10 Scavenger Hunts

Topic number 031 **Page 24-25**	*We all know how to "cluster" for writing ideas. What other activities or strategies can we use to select a subject?* (journal writing, free writing, listing, imaginary dialogue, etc.)
Topic number 102 **Page 51**	*How many different ways does* Writers INC *show you for combining sentences?* (10)
Topic number 118 **Page 61**	*The tour at Universal Studios is fun for everyone, but what does the writing term "universal" mean?* (a topic or an idea which applies to everyone)
Topic number 125 **Page 67**	*In writing to persuade, you write to prove a point or change someone's opinion. What other purpose is there?* (to clarify an issue)
Topic number 151 **Page 77** (Or: topic 339, page 157)	*What is plagiarism?* (the act of presenting someone else's ideas as your own)
Topic number 181 **Page 105**	*If you find the section on writing a paraphrase, you'll be able to paraphrase what a "paraphrase" is. What is it?* (A paraphrase is a restatement of someone else's ideas written in your own words.)
Topic number 198 **Page 113**	*In the reference section of the library or learning center, the* Information Please Almanac *is good for helping find what types of information, please?* (facts, statistics, and articles about that particular year)
Topic number 201 **Page 115**	*Look in the thesaurus section of your handbook for another word for "fear."* (timidity, panic, fright, etc.)
Topic number 205 **Page 119-120** (or: topic 343, pages 157 and 159)	*Are you well-versed in poetry? What is verse? What is poetry?* (Verse is a composition of rhythmic lines; poetry is verse that is a distinct work of thoughtful art.)
Topic number 231 **Page 133**	*The 5 W's and H are not the latest group of "rappers," but something used in writing news stories. What exactly are they?* (a questioning technique used to cover all bases in a news story: who, what, where, when, why, and how)

Topic number 235
Page 135

Can you abbreviate days and months in newspaper writing?
(You cannot abbreviate days; you can abbreviate months except May, June, and July.)

Topic number 427
Page 176

If you write a letter of application for a job, what kind of information should you include?
(your qualifications, personal data, and references)

Topic number 530
Page 240

If you recognize the parts before the whole, are you in your "right" mind, or is that a demonstration of left-brain thinking?
(left-brain thinking)

Topic number 542
Page 247

Which thinking operation is more complex—analysis or evaluation?
(evaluation)

Topic number 543
Page 248
(Or: topic 118, page 61)

What's the difference between inductive and deductive reasoning?
(Inductive reasoning leads from observed facts to a general conclusion; deductive starts with a general premise and applies it to a specific case.)

Topic number 546
Page 250

If you pile on the "qualifiers" in an argument, what are you doing to your argument?
(making your claim more flexible—almost, frequently, likely, etc.)

Topic number 601
Page 257

What is an ellipsis? Is that when the moon comes between the earth and sun, or is it something altogether different?
(An ellipsis is three periods used to show an omission or interruption.)

Topic number 697
Page 272

To capitalize or not to capitalize, that is the question.
What knowledge breaks as you open your handbook
to find the answers to the following within?
Do you capitalize the "un" in "un-American"?
Do you capitalize "winter"?
Do you capitalize "south" for the land of Robert E. Lee?
Do you capitalize "earth" for the ground you dig?
Do you capitalize on being asked by a "junior" to the "junior prom"?
(Correct answers: un, winter, South, earth, junior, Junior Prom)

Topic number 706
Page 274

If you send a postal letter to your uncle Mark in Hannibal, Missouri, what do you use for the abbreviation of Missouri?
(MO)

© Write Source, Box 460, Burlington, WI 53105

Topic number 706 **Page 274**	*MSG, BHT, and BHA are all approved food additives of the U.S. FDA, but what are PLZ, VLG, and RDG?* (abbreviations for plaza, village, and ridge)
Topic number 725 **Page 284**	*Is "alright" all right, or is it all wrong?* (all wrong—"all right" is correct)
Topic number 824 **Page 291**	*If you write in an essay that there are three "to's" in the English language, do you write it out as "to," "two," or "too"?)* (Nobody knows—it's one of the great writers' arguments of all time.)
Topic number 950 **Page 316**	*What sign letter is formed by making an "s" sign in the air?* (Z)
Topic number 952 **Page 317**	*If chickens get together and "brood," whales form a pod, and lions have a pride, then . . . Hey, hey! What are those monkeys walking down the street?* (a band)
Topic number 961 **Page 325**	*You're lost! You fell asleep and drifted for miles in your boat. But wait. Your compass settings are 24˚N latitude, 76˚W longitude. Where are you?* (the Bahamas)

Level 11 Scavenger Hunts

Topic number 023 **Page 17**	*What five steps does your handbook suggest you follow when you have very little time to revise your writing and find yourself "revising on the run"?* (1. Don't add any new information. 2. Remove unnecessary facts and details. 3. Find the best possible information and go with it. 4. Put the pieces in the best possible order. 5. Do what little rewriting is necessary.)
Topic number 028 **Page 20**	*What six things must the group members keep in mind when working in a writing group?* (1. Listen carefully. 2. Keep your comments positive and constructive. 3. Be specific. 4. Share your feelings. 5. Ask questions. 6. Add to what others say.)
Topic number 032 **Page 25**	*What six items from the "Essentials of Life Checklist" have you never written about?* (Answers will vary.)

Topic number 034
Page 28

Select a quotation from the sample writing topics in your hand-book and tell why you think it would be a good topic for you to write about.
(Answers will vary.)

Topic number 035
Page 30

Find the "Guidelines for Free Writing" in your handbook. Read the list of suggestions given and find two or more that you currently do NOT do when you free-write.
(Answers will vary.)

Topic number 062
Page 40

What is an incomplete comparison, and what can you do to make it complete?
(leaving out words which are necessary to make the sentence clear; simply complete the comparison)

Topic number 070
Page 42
(Or: topic 298, page 154)

What is a trite expression? Do you ever use any in your writing?
(flat, emotionless, overused words)

Topic number 115
Page 58

When writing an essay, how can you become a "three-eyed writer"?
(Open all three eyes in your head—your material eye to study your subject, your critical eye to check your thinking, and your intuitive eye to see how your reader will react to what you've written.)

Topic number 119
Page 62

Name three cliches you have personally read or heard used when someone was writing about a person.
(Answers will vary.)

Topic number 215
Pages 124-125

What seven steps are recommended by your handbook for writing about poetry?
(1. Paraphrase the poem. 2. Interpret the poem. 3. Examine the poem. 4. Evaluate the poem. 5. Compare the poem. 6. Read other poems. 7. Read related material.)

Topic number 244
Page 140

If you were asked to write an editorial, what type of "lead" would you use?
(Answers will vary. Information and example leads can be found at topic numbers 237 and 241.)

Topic number 256
Page 147

What six things should you NOT do in a book review?
(Refer to *Writers INC*.)

Topic number 258
Page 148

Which four questions (from the 18 listed) would you consider using if you kept a reading log the next time you read a book?
(Answers will vary.)

Topic number 324 **Page 156**	*What is a malapropism, and where did it come from?* (a type of pun or play on words which results when two words become jumbled in the speaker's mind; from the character Mrs. Malaprop)
Topic numbers **446-448** **Pages 187-192**	*If you had only the dictionary of prefixes, suffixes, and roots in your handbook to use, what would you say "neofracture" meant?* (state of being newly broken)
Topic number 471 **Page 206**	*One way to improve your test scores in science and history (or any other class) is to keep a learning log. What is a learning log, and what are three things you can include in it?* (A learning log is a type of writing journal in which you keep track of what's going on in a class. You might write about class activities, discuss new ideas and concepts, or evaluate your progress.)
Topic number 477 **Page 212**	*If you were asked to "justify" something on an essay exam, what would you do?* (tell why a position or point of view is good, right, or proper)
Topic number 509 **Page 230**	*What is a rhetorical question, and why would you ever use one?* (a question posed to emphasize a point, not to get an answer; rhetorical questions are often used in introductions or conclusions to get the reader or listener to stop and think)
Topic numbers **634, 640** **Pages 262, 263**	*How would you hyphenate great great grandfather? slow moving car? neatly arranged papers?* (great-great-grandfather, slow-moving car, neatly arranged papers)
Topic number 707 **Page 275**	*What do the following abbreviations stand for: TM, MST, COD, USSR?* (trademark, Mountain Standard Time, cash on delivery, Union of Soviet Socialist Republics)
Topic number 803 **Page 289**	*How do you know when to use the word "persons" rather than "people"?* (*People* refers to populations, races, and large groups; *persons* refers to individuals or human beings.)
Topic number 961 **Page 328**	*Houston, Texas, is farther south than Ciudad Juárez, Mexico. What other major U.S. cities are south of Ciudad Juárez?* (New Orleans, Miami, Tampa, Mobile)
Topic number 961 **Page 332**	*England is only one of four countries in the United Kingdom. What are the other three?* (Wales, Scotland, Northern Ireland)

Level 12 Scavenger Hunts

Topic number 010
Page 10

Name three of the seven suggestions offered in Writers INC *for writing an opening or lead paragraph.*
(a funny story, a challenge or puzzle, a quotation, etc.)

Topic number 013
Page 12

How many methods of development (ways to arrange your thoughts) does Writers INC *cover in the prewriting process?*
(eight)

Topic number 018
Page 15

What six questions can you ask during revising to help you escape the "badlands" of writing?
(Is your topic worn-out? Is your purpose stale? Is your voice predictable? Is your essay organized around an old formula? Does your first draft sound boring? Do your sentences fall into a rut?)

Topic number 123
Page 65

When you write about an event, what suggestions does your handbook offer?
(observe, investigate, describe, define, compare, speculate, evaluate, analyze . . .)

Topic number 410
Page 163

Why do businesses still write letters when it's so much easier and quicker just to call? In other words, what are some advantages of a written message over a spoken one?
(Letters can have more impact, they can be corrected before they are sent, they allow time to think, they provide a written reminder, etc.)

Topic number 417
Page 168

What are four familiar, worn-out expressions (expressions to avoid) when writing a business letter?
(above-mentioned, along this line, are in receipt of, please advise me, etc.)

Topic number 424
Page 173

What are some guidelines to follow in making your résumé the best that it can be?
(Put your name in capital letters centered on the top line, list career aims and objectives, include information on educational background, list job experiences, etc.)

Topic number 463
Page 199-200

What four major guidelines does Writers INC *suggest you follow when taking notes?*
(be attentive, be concise, be organized, be smart)

Topic number 465
Page 201

Cooperation is the key when working in a group. You probably already know that, but what can you do to become more actively involved when working in a group?
(listen well, propose ideas and opinions, challenge tactfully, and make good decisions)

Topic number 467
Page 202

In a group discussion, you certainly don't want to do all of the talking, so how can you encourage others to become involved?
(build trust, promote participation, maintain rapport)

Topic number 468
Page 203

With help from your classmates, find, study, and remember the 10 "Cooperative Group Skills."

Topic number 481
Page 215

It's just part of reality that sometimes you're judged on tests that you take. How can you learn to study for tests? What are some guidelines for reviewing and remembering test material?
(begin reviewing early, relate the material to your personal life, look for patterns, etc.)

Topic number 487
Pages 221-222

What are some recommended books that you should consider reading if you are planning to go to college?
(Answers will vary.)

Topic number 488
Pages 222-223

If college education is in your future, there are some things you need to know. What 10 tips does your Writers INC *offer to college freshmen?*
(tips on roommates, responsibility, budgeting, parents, studying, instructors, etc.)

Topic number 526
Page 237

Why do we think?
(We can't help it, we want to, we have to, we enjoy it, we need to.)

Topic number 530
Pages 239-240

Are you more right-brained or left-brained? How do you know?
(A right-brained person tends to be more creative; a left-brained person, more analytical or logical.)

Topic number 537
Pages 244-245

Thinking clearly does not come easily to all of us. What guidelines can you find in Writers INC *to help you get ready to think more clearly?*
(Clear and energize your mind, develop good learning habits, control the circumstances.)

Topic number 542
Page 247

If you are asked to break material down so that you can understand it better, what level of thinking operation are you being asked to perform?
(analysis)

Topic numbers **944-945** **Page 314**	*To avoid sexism when writing about occupations, what two main points should you consider?* (Don't use "man" words [foreman, chairman, etc.] or diminutive titles [steward, stewardess].)
Topic number 950 **Page 316**	*Phi Alpha Theta. You say that's Greek to you. What do these letters in the Greek alphabet look like?* (ΦΑΘ)
Topic number 958 **Page 322**	*How many feet deep is one fathom of water?* (6)
Topic number 961 **Page 325**	*If you traveled to 19˚S latitude and 174˚E longitude, where would you be?* (Fiji)
Topic number 961 **Page 328**	*The Bahamas are in what body of water?* (Atlantic Ocean)
Topic number 962 **Page 335**	*What was the first state to ratify the Constitution of the United States?* (Delaware)
Topic number 969 **Page 347**	*"Bit" is an acronym. What does the computer term "Bit" stand for?* (BInary digiT)

INClings: Over 140 Lessons to Use with *Writers INC*

Minilessons can transform any classroom into an active-learning environment. (We define a minilesson as anything that lasts about 10 minutes and covers a single idea or a basic core of knowledge.) Minilessons can be delivered from the front of the room and include the entire class. They can also be individualized or worked into cooperative learning groups. Ideally, each lesson will address a particular need—a need some students are experiencing right now. This makes learning much more meaningful and successful.

Implementation

Minilessons work very well in the writing workshop classroom. Those people who are "stuck" can be pulled together for 10 minutes each day until they solve their problem. Perhaps one group of students has a need to know how to punctuate Works Cited entries because they are finalizing research or I-Search papers. Another group of students may need practice combining sentences. And still another group needs time to develop their clustering skills. All this (and more) can be scheduled within one class period. The diverse needs of students can be met by teaching them the skills they need . . . when they need to learn them.

Approximately 30-35 minilessons are included at each level. They address many aspects of writing, reading, learning, and thinking covered in *Writers INC*.

Level 9 Minilessons

A ⬛ Happily Ever After . . . . *Revising*

Under the heading of "Revising" in *Writers INC* (topics **016-023**), find and read a section on "Opening and Closing Paragraphs."
>THINK of a story you've been wishing to tell somebody for quite some time.
>WRITE nothing of the story except a good last line.
>For fun, SHOW somebody else your last line and have them tell you (or write you) the story they think led up to it.

B ⬛ Really Bad Writing . . . . *Revising*

What are the "Badlands" of writing, as defined in the section on "Revising" in *Writers INC?* Just for fun,
>WRITE the first paragraph of a *really, really bad essay*, using the bad habits that good writers grow out of.
>OR . . . WRITE about your own experiences with revising—your method, a last-minute revision, advice to a younger writer, etc.

A 1 Time Bomb, 1 Red Pen .... *Prewriting: Listing*

In "Guidelines for Selecting a Subject," find a description of the technique of "Listing."

> PRETEND you've found a list on a scrap of paper in the street.
> WRITE the list in such a way that a reader can gather that it was written by a terrorist disguised as a high school teacher.
> OR, make up a character of your own and ask someone to guess the character's identity from the "Lost List" you write.

B Look What I Found .... *Prewriting: Found Ideas*

In "Guidelines for Selecting a Subject," find a description of "Found Writing Ideas."

> WRITE whatever comes to mind based on an idea that you discover in the room in which you are now sitting (or standing, or lying).
> For an extra challenge, TRY to find your idea by examining everything within an arm's length of your body.

C Butcher, Baker, Candlestick Maker .... *Selecting a Topic*

Find an "Essentials of Life Checklist" near the end of the "Guidelines for Selecting a Subject."

> CHOOSE one item from each of the four columns.
> MAKE UP four characters, each one associated with one of your four "essentials of life."
> BEGIN to write a story which includes all four characters.
> WRITE fast and freely for 5-8 minutes; then stop and jot down notes that will help you finish the story later.

D Dear Batman: .... *Selecting a Topic*

Find a two-page list of "Sample Writing Topics" (034) in *Writers INC*.

> PICK any topic that sparks your interest.
> PICK any name at random from the phone book.
> WRITE a letter about your chosen topic to your chosen person.
> INCLUDE the six parts of a letter explained in topic 411.

E O Rose, Thou Art Sick .... *Selecting a Topic*

Under "Sample Writing Topics" (034), find the list of "Descriptive" topics.

> PICK one person, one place, and one thing. (HINT: Pick a *weird* combination.)
> WRITE a poem in which the *person* talks about the *thing* in the *place*. (Can you imagine what your coach [person] would say about a monkey [thing] at a bowling alley [place]?)

A | Unless What? . . . . *Focused Free Writing*

Find and read the "Guidelines for Free Writing" (**035**) in *Writers INC*.
> WRITE the word "Unless" on a piece of paper and finish writing the sentence any way you can.
> CONTINUE writing sentences focused on the topic you started with. After 5 minutes,
> TRADE your work with someone else who's done the same thing.

B | Dear Diary . . . . *Writing with Style*

Browse through the section on "Writing with Style."
> IMAGINE you are somebody quite different from who you are: an astronaut, a Miss America candidate, an ax murderer, a cab driver, a dolphin trainer, etc.
> WRITE one page of that person's daily diary in the style you imagine that person would have. Make the style clearly different from your own.

C | It's a Dump, but It's Mine . . . . *Organizing Your Writing*

Read the section on "Methods of Organization" (**098**) in the chapter on "Writing Paragraphs" in *Writers INC*. Especially focus on the paragraph about "Order of Location."
> RECALL the layout of your bedroom at home.
> SUPPOSE you want to describe your room to a pen pal 800 miles away.
> DESCRIBE your bedroom in three short letters to your pen pal, first from the doorway to the farthest wall, then from the ceiling to the floor, and finally from your bed to the farthest corners.

D | Care and Keeping of a Turbolounge . . . . *Writing an Explanation*

Read the section in *Writers INC* on "Writing an Explanation" (**124**).
> INVENT a gizmo no one has ever heard of before.
> NAME it with a name no one has ever heard before.
> EXPLAIN to your partner exactly what the gizmo does and how it works.

A   Do You Mind If I Tape You? . . . . *The Interview*

In the chapter on "The Research Paper" find and read the sections on "Personalized Research" (**138**) and "Getting Involved" (**139**).

> RESEARCH the Korean or Vietnam War, a foreign country, or a major theme park like Disney World by finding somebody who was there.
>
> INTERVIEW the person, asking all the questions a curious person would want to ask.
>
> TAKE NOTES or TAPE-RECORD the interview.
>
> WRITE DOWN the best parts of the interview in dialogue form (see topic **136**); connect the sections of dialogue with your own explanations, comments, and interpretations.

B   Numbers, Dates, and Names . . . . *Parts of a Book*

Review the description of "Parts of a Book" in *Writers INC* (**200**).

> TURN to the copyright page of *Writers INC*.
>
> WRITE down the ISBN number for the softcover edition of this book.
>
> Also WRITE the earliest copyright date and the name of the earlier edition of *Writers INC*.

C   Croak / Cash In / Kick the Bucket . . . . . . *Using the Thesaurus*

Read the instructions for "Using the Thesaurus" in *Writers INC* (**201**).

> CHOOSE one of the following pairs of words: live/die, sober/drunk, build/ destroy.
>
> LOOK UP both words in a thesaurus and
>
> STUDY the words listed under each.
>
> WRITE a paragraph explaining the differences you notice between the positive vocabulary and the negative one.

D   Grammar, Dahling . . . . *Using the Dictionary*

Read the section on "Using the Dictionary" in *Writers INC* (**202**). Reread the short section on "Etymology."

> LOOK UP the etymology of the word "GRAMMAR" in an excellent dictionary.
>
> LOOK UP the etymology of the word "GLAMOUR."
>
> WRITE an essay in answer to the question "What do *grammar* and *glamour* have in common?"

A | Red Rover, Red Rover .. *Writing the Poem: A Jump-rope Jingle*

Read the opening ("The Poet in You") to the chapter on "Writing the Poem."
> REMEMBER a jump-rope jingle or a playground chant from your childhood.
> ADD a new stanza to the old jingle.
> SHARE your jingle with a partner.

B | Start from Scratch .... *Writing a Poem about Nothing*

Read "Always Write a Poem Like This" (**216**).
> WRITE your own brief poem about having nothing to write.

C | Once Upon a Harley .... *Pass-Along Stories*

Read topic **221** of *Writers INC*, which offers some basic instructions for constructing a plot.
> THINK how you would tell a modern-day version of *Cinderella*.
> FORM a circle with your class.
> WRITE the first sentence of your version on a piece of paper as everyone else does the same.
> PASS your paper to the person next to you.
> WRITE a second sentence on the sheet your neighbor passes to you. Try to catch the spirit of your partner's story and keep it going.
> CONTINUE adding sentences and passing papers until your own sheet goes all around the circle and comes back to you.

D | Tell Me About Yourself .... *Writing a Bio-Poem*

Read the instructions for writing a "Bio-Poem" under topic **259**, "More Than Mere Words."
> CHOOSE a partner from your class.
> INTERVIEW each other until you have the information you need to complete a bio-poem.
> WRITE a bio-poem about your partner.

E | Money Back Guarantee .... *Letter of Complaint*

Read the sample "Letter of Complaint" (**416**) in *Writers INC*.
> PRETEND you are the Customer Service Manager who received the letter about Ralph Bettner's TV.
> WRITE a courteous and helpful business reply to Mr. Bettner.
> USE exactly the same letter format that Bettner used.

A Reading and Remembering . . . . *Improving Reading and Vocabulary*

Suppose you are in a Big Brother or Big Sister program and your Little Brother (or Sister), named Pat, writes you a letter saying he (or she) is having trouble reading and remembering things in school.

> TURN to *Writers INC* and survey the contents of the chapter on "Improving Reading and Vocabulary," looking for good advice to pass along.
>
> WRITE a personal letter to Pat, giving him (or her) your best advice for reading better and remembering more in school.

B Dear Chris: . . . . *Writing a Letter*

Find the illustration you like best in *Writers INC*.

> WRITE a letter to the illustrator, Chris Krenzke, telling him which illustration you like and why you like it.
>
> USE "semi-block" form for your letter as it is described in the section on "Letters, Memos, and Résumés" (**411**).

C Watch My Eyeballs . . . . *Translating Words into Thoughts*

Find the section on "Translating Words into Thoughts" in the *Reading and Learning* section (**450**).

> CHOOSE a partner; read section **450**.
>
> LET your partner watch your eyeballs as you read and count the stops ("fixations") for each line.
>
> WATCH your partner's eyeballs as he or she reads, COUNT the number of fixations, and
>
> COMPARE to see who has the least number of fixations per line.

D FLAB . . . . *Cooperative Group Skills: Writing a Memo*

Suppose you belong to a local chapter of a national group called "Future Leaders Acting Big" (FLAB). The problem is that everybody in your group yaks at once and no one listens; everyone wants to be a leader and no one wants to be led. Finally, out of exasperation, you decide to act really big and *write a memo!*

> READ the sections on "Cooperative Group Skills" in *Writers INC* (**465-467**).
>
> STUDY the guidelines for "Writing Memorandums" (**419**).
>
> WRITE a memo to all the members of FLAB, briefly summarizing what the group needs to know about group dynamics.

A | Captain's Log · · · · · · · · · · · · · · · · · *Keeping a Learning Log*

Carefully read the "Guidelines to Keeping a Learning Log" in *Writers INC* (**471**).
> START a learning log for the class in which you use *Writers INC* the most.
> For your first entry, WRITE "Guidelines" followed by today's date.
> Then CHOOSE your favorite one of the twelve guidelines and follow it.

B | Life on Zurk · *Using Commas*

Imagine another planet, called Zurk, in which the noble race of Silicos always frap their trunyons until their keestors blavel.
> STUDY all the sentences in topics **605-619** which demonstrate the correct use of commas.
> REWRITE each one of the model sentences so that it reveals something new about life on Zurk. ("My friend smokes constantly, but he still condemns industry for its pollution."
> REVISED: Grebnar's pet snard trenkles constantly, but it still foreslavers trimsap with its bellyasters.)
> (SUGGESTION: Do this exercise with a partner, take turns inventing sentences.)

C | Siamese Sentences · · · · · · · · · · · · · · · · · *Using Semicolons*

Study the rules for proper use of the semicolon (**620-623**).
> READ topic **526**, "Why Do We Think?" and topic **527**, "A Thinking Attitude."
> FIND at least six pairs of sentences on that page which could be joined with a semicolon.
> WRITE OUT the combined sentences, punctuating them correctly.

D | Simply Dashing · *Using the Dash*

Study topics **631** and **632** in *Writers INC* to learn the proper uses of the dash.
> RECALL an exciting movie you've seen or an absorbing book you've read.
> IMITATE the model sentences, writing about the movie or book you've chosen.
> USE dashes correctly and expressively in your imitations.

E | Gimme That · · · · · · · · *Using Quotation Marks and Apostrophes*

Look over the rules for using quotation marks (**649-657**) and apostrophes (**668-675**) in "Re-Marks: A Proofreader's Guide."
> REMEMBER a time from your childhood when you and your brothers and sisters or friends were arguing over whose toys were whose.
> WRITE the argument as you imagine it would have sounded.
> In your paragraphs and passages of dialogue, USE quotation marks and apostrophes correctly.

A So to Speak .... *Using Quotation Marks*

Study the rules for using quotation marks in topic **652**.
> THINK of a distinctive word, slang or otherwise, which one of your friends always uses.
> WRITE a sentence about your friend in which you use the word in a special way.
> USE quotation marks properly to draw attention to the special use.

B Test Case .... *Capitalization*

Review the rules for capitalization (**685-697**) in *Writers INC*.
> CHOOSE a partner.
> WRITE a paragraph to present to your partner as a test.
> In your paragraph, USE a variety of words that should be capitalized but reduce all capitals to lowercase for your partner to correct.
> EXCHANGE tests with your partner and evaluate both of them when you are finished.

C Headroom .... *Forming Plural Nouns*

Review the rules for forming plural nouns (**698-705**).
> VISUALIZE one of the rooms in your house and all the objects in it.
> LIST as many of the objects as you can remember. Beside each word on your list write its correct plural form.
> If in doubt about the form, CHECK a dictionary.

D Freeze-Dried Sentences .... *Common Abbreviations*

Note the list of "Common Abbreviations" in *Writers INC* (**707**).
> TRANSLATE the following sentence into plain English by writing out the abbreviated words:
>> *R.S.V.P. to the PTA (c/o D.A.) or the BBB hdqrs. ASAP w/ misc. illus. lit. about, e.g., the GNP of the USSR, the IQ of VIP's, or the avg. m.p.g. of those w/ M.A. degrees in zool.*
> MAKE UP your own sentence using a different set of abbreviations from the list.

A | Animal Crackers . . . . *Understanding Grammar*

Review the definition and examples of *nouns* in the chapter "Understanding Grammar" (**841-848**). Focus on topic **844** for a definition of "collective noun."

DO you know the wonderful collective nouns used to name groups of the following animals?

bears	*goats*	*swans*
cats	*geese*	*whales*
chickens	*lions*	*foxes*

LOOK UP all of these collective nouns in a chart called "Animal Crackers" (*Writers INC*, Appendix, topic **952**).

CHOOSE three of the collective nouns that you like the best.

COMPOSE interesting sentences using the collective nouns in their correct senses.

B | Beyond Awesome, Different, and Cool . . . . *Understanding "Degrees"*

Study topic **885** and the table in topic **887** showing "positive," "comparative," and "superlative" degrees of adjectives and adverbs.

THINK of three television shows you've watched—one good, one better, and one best.

SUPPOSE you asked three friends what they thought of the best one. One said it was "Awesome"; another said it was "Different"; and the third said it was "Cool."

Not satisfied, you WRITE your own critique, comparing the three shows.

USE the three degrees of adjectives and adverbs effectively in your "review."

C | Prepositional Poem . . . . *Using Prepositions*

Consult the list of prepositions in "Re-marks," topic **892**.

COMPOSE a poem of at least eight lines, on any subject, in which each line begins with a different preposition.

TRADE poems with a partner and read your poems aloud.

DISCUSS what your respective poems mean.

D | One Hand Washes the Other . . . . *Symbols of Correction*

See the "Symbols of Correction" on the inside back cover of *Writers INC*.

With a partner, EXCHANGE papers you wrote earlier this year for any of your classes.

EDIT your partner's paper, using the correction symbols wherever possible.

ADD a written comment which conveys your *personal* response to your partner's paper as a whole.

Level 10 Minilessons

A **Kissing at Angles** .... *Audience*

What are three basic "angles of vision" in a writer's address to a reader? (Check out the section on "Revising" in *Writers INC*.)
> WRITE an extended definition of "kissing" for 1) a kindergarten class, 2) a senior in high school, and 3) a panel of family physicians.

B **A "Bad" Time Was Had by All** .... *Levels of Diction*

Find a reference to three different "levels of diction" in the section on "Revising" in *Writers INC*.
> REWRITE an article from a local or student newspaper in the wildest, hippest *slang* you know.

C **Cluster Clusters** .... *Clustering*

Find a diagram which illustrates a prewriting technique called "clustering."
> READ the instructions for clustering and study the diagram.
> CREATE your own cluster around the nucleus word "clustering."
> WRITE a short essay about your own creative thinking process, taking off from your cluster around the term "clustering."

D **Ah Jist Larned** .... *Prewriting: Sentence Completion*

In "Guidelines for Selecting a Subject," find and read the instructions for "Sentence Completion."
> FINISH one of the sample sentences started there for you.
> Just for practice in writing dialogue, WRITE your sentence a second time in a voice with a distinctive *accent*.

E **Read My Lips** .... *How to . . . ?*

Under "Sample Writing Topics" (**034**), see the list of "Expository" topics.
> CHOOSE a topic from the "How to" section, or make up one of your own.
> TELL a classmate how to do whatever the topic is.
> When you're done, DISCUSS with a classmate how you would give instructions to someone from another country who doesn't speak much English.
> OR . . . Tell a classmate who pretends to be from another country.

A | **Why Do We Get Pimples?** . . . . *Writing Explanations*

Under "Sample Writing Topics" (**034**), find the list of "Expository" topics.
> CHOOSE a topic under "The causes of . . . ."
> PRETEND you are a kindergartner and WRITE a kindergartner's explanation of the cause.

B | **A Race Between Education and Catastrophe** . . . . *Quotations*

Under "Sample Writing Topics" (**034**) find a list of thought-provoking quotations.
> CHOOSE one of the quotations you like most.
> WRITE a note to somebody in your class explaining what the quotation means to you.

C | **PERLFUNCCREEXPPERV** . . . . *A Survey of Writing Forms*

With a partner, make a list of all the different kinds of writing you've done in the past year (letter to Cousin Zelda, grocery list, book report, etc.).
> FIND and STUDY the "Survey of Writing Forms" at the end of the chapter on "The Writing Process."
> MARK each item on your list when you decide whether it is PERL (personal), FUNC (functional), CRE (Creative), EXP (expository), or PERV (persuasive).

D | **"The Abyss" Was, Like, What a Scream!** . . . . *Writing Style*

Under "Improving Sentence Style" in *Writers INC,* find and read the section "Smooth & Graceful." Pay special attention to topic **076**, "Mixed Construction."
> FIND a partner and TALK together about the most recent movie that you both have seen.
> LISTEN carefully to the sentences your partner speaks and
> WRITE down any mixed constructions you hear. (*Tip*: Try tape-recording your conversation, playing it back, and making a transcript.)
> TRY to write unmixed versions of those sentences.

E | **First I Was Born** . . . . *Outlining*

Read the sections on outlining in *Writers INC* (**110-113**).
> CUT or TEAR a sheet of paper into 15-20 thin strips.
> On each of three or four strips, WRITE a sentence about a major turning point in your life.
> On the remaining strips, WRITE complete sentences expressing important ideas about those turning points.
> ORGANIZE the strips into outline form on the desk or table in front of you.
> IMAGINE how you would use the outline to compose your own autobiography.

A Gas Lines . . . . *Using an Outline*

Read the traditional essay, "America—The Land of Plenty?" (**116**).
> FOCUS on the last paragraph, which closes with a prediction of the future . . .
> which we live in now.
> WRITE a sentence outline (**113**) for an essay in which you explore the attitude
> of Americans toward energy consumption today.

B According to a Tree House . . . . *Voice in Writing*

Under "Writing About a Place" in *Writers INC* (**120**), read the list of possible
topics.
> CHOOSE one that grabs you, or choose a place from the secret list in your
> mind.
> READ suggestion #2: "Investigate." Well, what *if* a place could talk?
> START WRITING in the voice of your place.

C -Ism That Something . . . . *Writing an Extended Definition*

Find and read the section in *Writers INC* on "Writing a Definition" (**122**).
> CHOOSE an -ism you know something about—communism, patriotism,
> Catholicism, hypnotism, etc.
> WRITE a formal definition like the one under topic **122**. Use a dictionary if
> you wish.
> Now, JOT DOWN further details you could use in a definition essay. Think
> about examples, stories, events, people, sayings, places, objects, books,
> etc.

D Getting to the Root . . . . *Building Vocabulary*

Read the guidelines for "Writing a Definition" in *Writers INC* (**122**).
> TURN to the "Dictionary of Prefixes" (**446**), "Suffixes" (**447**), and "Roots"
> (**448**).
> WRITE a reasonable-sounding definition for each of the following make-
> believe words, after consulting the "Dictionary of Prefixes, Suffixes, and
> Roots":

amphidictive	*micromorphosteoid*	*similcalorizoic*
perfractacardiology	*retrojectophobia*	*philidiocapticule*
submatrifumalgia	*pseudopolyacergastrorhea*	*presolidentomy*

> PUT together your own words and challenge the class to write a definition
> for each.

A | Git Yer Red Hots Right Here . . . . *Writing to Persuade*

Study the section "Writing to Persuade" in *Writers INC* (**125**).
  With a partner, DECIDE on some product you'd like to persuade people to
    buy (a certain brand of shoe, perfume, or tennis racket).
  Let one of you CREATE a magazine ad appealing purely to emotion.
  Let the other ARGUE logically that people should buy the product.
  DECIDE which approach is more persuasive.

B | Short Stuff . . . . *Writing a Précis*

Study the section on "The Précis" (**182**) in the chapter on "Writing Summaries."
  CHOOSE an interesting short section from one of your textbooks for a class
    other than English.
  WRITE a précis of it, using the "Guidelines for Writing a Précis."

C | Poetically Ever After . . . . . *Where Short Story & Poem Overlap*

Read the section "Where Short Story and Poem Overlap" (**206**).
  TELL your class one of your favorite fables, fairy tales, or horror stories.
  WRITE a poem telling the same story in a different way.
  TRADE poems with a partner and discuss what you've tried to do in your
    poem.

D | Genius Born to Humble Parents . . . . . *Writing the News Story*

Read the chapter in *Writers INC* on "Writing the News Story" (**230-238**).
  WRITE a brief but complete news article, with headline, which reports your
    own birth as a newsworthy event.

E | Inverted Pyramid . . . . *Inverted-Pyramid Structure*

Read the glossary of "Journalism Terms" in *Writers INC* (**246**).
  REREAD the definition of "Inverted-Pyramid Structure."
  STUDY the following sentences:
    1. According to the hunters, a smell like that of "burnt hair" lingered in
       the area.
    2. Humboldt was not available for comment.
    3. The ring was first discovered by pheasant hunters last Friday.
    4. The flattened circle in Bill Humboldt's oat field was caused by the
       thrusters of an alien space vehicle, said local authorities last night.
  REORDER the sentences in inverted-pyramid structure.

A | Feedback . . . . *Writing about Literature*

Read the chapter on "Writing about Literature," paying special attention to any sections on book reviewing (**250, 253, 255-258**).

      GATHER together your knowledge of, impressions of, and responses to *Writers INC*.

      WRITE a one-page book review of *Writers INC*.

      SEND a copy of your review to FEEDBACK, The Write Source, Box 460, Burlington, WI 53105.

B | Figuratively Speaking . . . . *Figures of Speech*

Read closely the definitions for ten types of "Figures of Speech" (**313**) in the list of "Literary Terms."

      THINK of one of the best athletes or musicians or actors at your school.

      WRITE ten sentences about that person and his or her way of performing, each sentence containing a different one of the ten figures of speech. (Be sure your figures are original ones, not cliches—see topic **287**.)

C | Going Phrazy . . . . *Verbal Phrases*

Read the section on "Writing-to-Learn Activities" (**473**). Also study topic **912,** which explains the three types of verbal phrases: *gerund, infinitive,* and *participle.*

      SUPPOSE you've been asked to give brief comments about "Writing-to-Learn" activities at a conference for young writers like yourself.

      WRITE *three* drafts of your prepared comments.

      In the 1st draft, USE *no* verbal phrases at all.

      In the 2nd draft, USE *two* gerund phrases, *two* infinitive phrases, and *two* participial phrases.

      In the 3rd draft, USE any number (more than zero) and any type of verbal phrases you want.

      REREAD your drafts.

      WRITE a short note to your writing teacher explaining which draft you like best and why.

D | Sixties Speech . . . . *Speaking: Stylistic Devices*

In the chapter on "Speech Skills," find the "Student Commentary" (**511**).

      NOTICE the stylistic devices labeled in the right margin.

      READ the student commentary.

      UNDERLINE the phrases or sentences in the commentary which are referred to in the margin.

A Pardon My Inflection .... *Speaking Terms*

Find a glossary of "Speech Terms" in *Writers INC* (**524**).
> FIND a term in the list which you don't know well.
> READ the definition.
> USE the word accurately in a sentence, WRITE the sentence on paper, and
> SPEAK it to your partner.

B Growth Rings .... *Thinking Phases: A Self-Analysis*

Read about "Thinking Phases" in *Writers INC* (**531**).
> WRITE a journal entry in which you think back through the years of your
> life.
> IDENTIFY the stages of your own development as a thinker.

C If I Were My Shoe .... *The Creative Mind in Action*

Read the description of "The Creative Mind in Action" (**536**).
> CHOOSE an ordinary object other than a No. 2 pencil—your shoe, a piece of
> chalk, a book, a key, etc.
> ACTIVATE your imagination by applying the steps in the box ("The No. 2
> Pencil Meets a Creative Mind") to your chosen subject.
> ADD a few imaginative twists of your own.
> JOT DOWN phrases and sentences to capture your thoughts.
> (*TIP*: Use a thesaurus to find more emotionally loaded words; see topic **201**.)

D Fallout .... *Using a Colon*

Read the model sentence which shows how to use a colon to introduce a list
(**627**).
> SUPPOSE your locker, your knapsack, or your purse fell open and spilled its
> contents on the floor.
> WRITE a sentence which uses a colon to introduce the long list of junk items
> a passerby might see.

E Careful .... *Using Parentheses*

Study the rules for using parentheses in topic **662** of *Writers INC*.
> THINK of a dangerous procedure you've done—rock climbing, lighting a
> barbecue grill, cleaning gutters, cutting open an English muffin, etc.
> WRITE a paragraph instructing someone like yourself how to perform the
> operation safely.
> PLACE appropriate warnings and cautions in parentheses.

A ▌ All Ready, Already . . . . *Using the Right Word*

In the chapter "Using the Right Word" (**715-837**), search the list of often-confused word pairs for five pairs that sometimes confuse you.
> READ the samples where both (or three) terms are used in the same sentence.
> PUT the book away and
> COMPOSE five sample sentences of your own, each correctly employing a different set of contrasted terms.

B ▌ Dear, Deer . . . . *Using the Right Word*

Scan the long list of commonly confused word pairs in the chapter "Using the Right Word" (**715-837**).
> WRITE a half page about any subject you choose. In your writing,
> USE as many *wrong* words as you can from the list of mistaken pairs.
> EXCHANGE papers with a partner.
> USE appropriate symbols from the "Symbols of Correction" listed inside the back cover of *Writers INC* to point out and correct your partner's "errors."

C ▌ Ladders of Concrete . . . . *General and Specific Nouns*

Some nouns are general, some are more specific, and some are highly specific. You can form a "ladder of specification" by putting words in increasing order of concreteness. For example, mammal—biped—human—male—male rock star—Mick Jagger.
> BUILD "ladders of specificity" starting from these general terms. (If three steps seems too easy, try five!)

> > *machine*   *motion*   *group*   *material*

> WRITE a short paragraph using mostly words from the general end of the "ladder."
> WRITE a second paragraph replacing the general words with specific ones.
> TRADE paragraphs with a partner.
> WRITE a third paragraph explaining which one of your partner's paragraphs you like better and why.

© Write Source, Box 460, Burlington, WI 53105

A   Stand-Ins .... *Pronouns and Antecedents*

Study the section on pronouns (**849-868**).
> FIND a passage in a paper you've written that has a variety of pronouns in it.
> CIRCLE each pronoun.
> DRAW a line from each pronoun to its antecedent (**850**).
> DRAW a box around the antecedent; if there is no clear antecedent, check whether the pronoun is accurately used.

B   I Get a Kick Out of This .... *Active and Passive Verbs*

Review the definitions of *active* and *passive* verbs in *Writers INC* (**872 & 877**).
> CHOOSE a sport which involves hitting or kicking a ball.
> WRITE a paragraph describing a moment of intense action in that sport from the point of view of one of the players; use *active* verbs.
> REWRITE the paragraph, describing the same action from the point of view of the ball; use *passive* verbs.

C   In Praise of the Phrase.............. *Gerund, Infinitive, and Participial Phrases*

Study the definitions of *gerund, infinitive,* and *participial* phrases in *Writers INC* (**912**).
> READ the following short sentences:
> > 1. I study a map.
> > 2. We take a vacation.
> > 3. We camp in a tent.
> CONVERT each of the three short sentences into, first, a gerund phrase, second, an infinitive phrase, and third, a participial phrase.
> After doing that, COMPLETE each sentence with its phrase in a proper place.

D   Sharp Clauses .... *Independent and Dependent Clauses*

Read the description of *independent* and *dependent* clauses in *Writers INC* (**916**).
> CONSULT the list of "Sample Writing Topics" (**034**).
> SELECT a topic under the heading "Persuasive."
> WRITE two closely related sentences about that topic.
> CIRCLE the one you want to emphasize the most.
> COMBINE the two sentences into one by using the circled sentence as your *main clause.*
> USE a subordinating conjunction (see **897** for a list) to turn your other sentence into a *subordinate clause.*
> CHOOSE another topic and REPEAT the process.

A | Trips and Troops, Clutches and Clowders .... *Agreement of Subject and Verb*

Study topic **926**, which describes when to use collective nouns with singular verbs and when to use them with plural verbs.

> CHOOSE one or more of the collective nouns from the "Animal Crackers" chart (**952**).
>
> For each collective noun you choose, WRITE one sentence using a singular verb and one using a plural verb.

B | Planetary Conclusions .... *Thinking Logically*

See the chart of the solar system and the table labeled "Planet Profusion" (**953**) in the appendix to *Writers INC*.

> READ the paragraph about our solar system.
>
> WRITE a paragraph to follow the first one.
>
> To compose your paragraph, STATE and DISCUSS any interesting conclusions you draw from the numbers in the table.
>
> WRITE a "thinking" paragraph explaining what logic you used to draw conclusions from the table.

C | Sign Design .... *Inductive Reasoning*

Look up "Inductive Reasoning" in the index of *Writers INC* and read the sections listed there.

> APPLY inductive reasoning to the display of "Traffic Signs" and "Service and Guide Signs" (**957**) as follows:
>
> STUDY the colors, shapes, images, and words you see on the signs;
>
> TRY to conclude exactly why each sign appears as it does. To demonstrate your conclusions,
>
> SUPPOSE you are in charge of "sign design" for the Dept. of Transportation (DOT).
>
> WRITE a memorandum (see **419**) giving your employees a set of general design rules that would produce signs exactly like these. For example, "All signs that warn against possibly fatal mistakes must contain bright red." (Do any signs seem to defy your rules?)

Level 11 Minilessons

A | **Samuel Who?** . . . . *Thoughts on Writing*

Under the heading of "Focusing Your Efforts" in the "Prewriting Section" of *Writers INC*, find out who said, "The two most engaging powers of an author are to make new things familiar and familiar things new."

WRITE a short interpretation of what this sentence means.

LOOK UP the name of this author in a good encyclopedia or biographical dictionary and find out why this author is still remembered.

B | **Hello. Do I Know You?** . . . . *Writing the First Draft*

Under the heading of "Writing the First Draft" in *Writers INC*, find the statement, "Your writing is one-half of a conversation with a reader you invent."

READ and UNDERSTAND the sentence in its context.

IMAGINE and WRITE a "Bob Newhart" conversation, i.e., a telephone conversation in which you hear only one person speaking. (The deadpan comedian Bob Newhart made this technique famous in his hilarious TV routines.)

(*Tip:* Try a conversation with an unheard person on the other end who brings unbelievable news or who makes stupid or impossible demands.)

C | **Economical Prose** . . . . *Revising*

Under the heading of "Revising" in *Writers INC*, find out who wrote the epigraph, ". . . there are days when the result is so bad that no fewer than five revisions are required. In contrast, when I'm greatly inspired, only four revisions are needed."

RESEARCH and WRITE: Visit the library and find a fairly recent article by this author. Write a one-paragraph summary of it. (Since the author is a famous economist, an exercise in economical prose writing seems appropriate!)

D | **Yo, Gorby** . . . . *Prewriting: Imaginary Dialogue*

In "Guidelines for Selecting a Subject," find and read the instructions for writing an "Imaginary Dialogue."

IMAGINE and WRITE a dialogue between yourself and a major world leader about a current world situation you care about.

(SUGGESTION: In another class or at home, RESEARCH the problem by reading about it in a newspaper or weekly newsmagazine.)

A License to Kill? .... *Using Reasons*

In the chapter on "Writing Paragraphs" in *Writers INC*, find the section on "Types of Paragraphs" (**093-096**).
> READ carefully the paragraph on capital punishment.
> DRAW a line down the middle of a blank sheet of paper.
> In the left column, LIST the paragraph's major reasons for abolishing capital punishment.
> In the right column, WRITE down a solid objection to each of the reasons in the left column.
> WRITE your reaction to what you have just done at the bottom of the page.

B The Ghost of Kamal .... *Beginning Your Essay*

Read the creative essay, "Why Did Kamal Die?" (**117**).
> WRITE the beginning of the essay in a new way, as if the story were being told by the ghost of Kamal.
> THINK up another creative approach to an essay on world hunger and describe it to a partner.

C Obituary .... *Writing a Précis*

Read "Why Did Kamal Die?" in the section on "The Creative Essay" (**117**).
> REVIEW the "Guidelines for Writing a Précis" (**182**).
> Without rereading the Kamal essay, write a précis of it.
> CHECK your précis against the original for accuracy.

D The Real Ronald McDonald .... *Writing About a Person*

Under "Writing About a Person" (**119**), read through the list of possible topics.
> CHOOSE one, then
> SCAN the list of suggestions (#1-8), and
> JOT DOWN notes under as many of the headings as you can.
> CONSIDER how you might develop your notes into an essay.

E Twenty-Four Karat Heart .... *Avoiding Cliches*

Under "Writing About a Person" (**119**), read the list of cliches to be avoided.
> CHOOSE one of the cliches and write a creative new version that makes those dead bones get up and dance. For example, change *heart of gold* to *the heart of Mother Theresa* or *a 24-karat heart*.

A One Strike, You're Out . . . . *Understanding Plagiarism*

In the chapter on "The Research Paper," read the comments on the meaning of **plagiarism** (**151**).
> STUDY the guidelines on "Writing to Persuade" (**125**).
> SUPPOSE you were in a debate on the topic, "Resolved: Students who plagiarize on a paper should automatically fail the unit."
> TAKE one side or the other (pro or con) in the debate and try to persuade the other side of your view.
> ADD one fact from a published source which is not common knowledge in that field.

B Inner Independence . . . . *Reflective Thinking*

In the chapter on "The Research Paper," under the heading "Your Responsibility as a Researcher," notice the epigraph (quotation) from Doris Lessing (**150**).
> READ the quotation.
> REFLECT on its meaning, especially the meaning of the phrase "inner independence."
> WRITE an exploratory essay revealing your understanding of the term "inner independence."
> USE any one of the "Methods of Organization" (**098**) to develop your essay.

C Love Ya, Babe (You Dirty Rat) . . . . *Writing Between the Lines*

Read the "Anatomy of a Short Story Writer" (**219**). Focus especially on the paragraph labeled "Ear."
> LISTEN carefully to the speech of someone who does not realize he or she is being overheard.
> DIVIDE a sheet with a line down the middle.
> To the left of this line WRITE down a snatch of the person's speech as accurately as you can.
> To the right of the line WRITE the "subtext" of the person's speech—the *real* thoughts (as well as you can determine them) which the speaker never expresses in so many words.

D Spreading *Writers INC* . . . . *Writing the Editorial*

Turn in *Writers INC* to the chapter on "Writing the News Story" and read two sections: "The Structure of an Editorial" (**243**) and "Writing the Editorial" (**244**).
> PRETEND your classroom has a newspaper and you are the editor.
> DECIDE how you would like *Writers INC* to be used in your classroom.
> WRITE a 100-200 word editorial proposing a better way to use *Writers INC*.
> (Suggestion: If you are in an English class, try editorializing about using *Writers INC* in your history, biology, or some other class.)

A | How Many Feet in Your Name? . . . . *Literary Terms: Poetry*

In the list of "Literary Terms: Poetry" in *Writers INC* (**343**), study the definition of the term "Foot" and the six types of poetic feet listed below it.

> WRITE your own name on a piece of paper.
>
> MARK the stressed (´) syllables in your name (En´gelbert | Hum´ perdinck), placing a vertical line between the metric feet if your name is more than three syllables long.
>
> WRITE down the name of the type of metric feet in your name (Hum´perdinck = dactylic).

B | Bad Business . . . . *Expressions to Avoid in Business Letters*

Read the letter by Ralph Bettner to the Customer Service Manager at Telmar, Inc., which you'll find under topic **416** of *Writers INC*.

> LOOK THROUGH the list of "Expressions to Avoid in Business Writing" (**417**).
>
> REWRITE Ralph Bettner's fine letter, but make it really, really bad this time by using lots of expressions one ought to avoid.
>
> OR . . . WRITE a letter of complaint recounting a defective product you once got stuck with.

C | State Your Claim . . . . *Key Stages in Formal Argument*

Study the three types of claims described in the "Key Stages in the Formal Argument" (**545**).

> For each of the following topics, WRITE DOWN one claim of *fact*, one claim of *value*, and one claim of *policy*:
>
> > *movies   smoking   sex education   sports   pets   driving*

D | World's Greatest Job . . . . *Letters of Application*

Read the sample "Letter of Application" in *Writers INC* and the guidelines above it (**427**).

> SUPPOSE there is one opening for the position of "substitute teacher" to cover for your teacher when he or she is absent.
>
> SUPPOSE all the others in your class are applying for the job, since there are no minimum educational requirements and the pay is phenomenal ($24/class).
>
> WRITE a letter of application *so good* that you are certain to get the job.

A | Writing to Learn . . . . *Dramatic Scenarios*

Find a discussion of "Writing-to-Learn Activities" in *Writers INC* (**473**). Focus on #3, "Dramatic Scenarios."

> CHOOSE a class other than your English class, whichever one interests you the most.
> CHOOSE a famous person in that field (Mozart, Einstein, Napoleon, Plato, etc.).
> READ about that person in an encyclopedia or other book.
> CHOOSE an important moment in that person's life.
> WRITE your imagining of that person's thoughts at the crucial moment on that crucial day.

B | Test Yourself . . . . *Understanding the Essay Test*

Find the chapter in *Writers INC* on "Taking Tests." Focus especially on topics **476** and **477**, "Understanding the Essay Test Question" and "Key Words."

> FIND a paragraph in one of your textbooks (other than English) which is filled with interesting information.
> READ over the paragraph several times.
> WRITE an essay test question to which the paragraph you chose would be an excellent answer.

C | Ad Appeal . . . . *Speaking: Persuasive Appeals*

In the chapter on "Speech Skills," find the section titled "A Closer Look at Style" (**496-510**). Read the short excerpts from speeches by John F. Kennedy and notice the types of "Appeal" (printed in blue) which they exemplify.

> FIND a major weekly newsmagazine.
> STUDY the full-page advertisements in it.
> WRITE a list of the different appeals you detect in the ads.

D | Oh Captain, My Captain . . . . *Speaking: Marking the Text*

Find the box showing how to mark the text of a speech for oral interpretation (**518**).

> FIND a poem in *Writers INC* or in another book.
> SUPPOSE you are expected to read the poem before a large audience.
> MARK the text of the poem with appropriate symbols for an expressive reading.
> READ the poem to a partner in class, following your own markings for expression.
> DISCUSS your reading with your partner and revise your markings accordingly.

A   Hank and Frank .... *Thinking in Dialogue*

Read the section on "A Thinking Attitude" in the chapter on "The Thinking Process" (**527**). Figure out the difference between Hank and Frank.

SUPPOSE Hank and Frank have an argument about whether the U.S. should permit the death penalty.

WRITE a dialogue between Hank and Frank which shows the difference between their respective ways of thinking.

(*TIP:* For a model dialogue, see "You Ain't Nothin' But a Hound Dog," **136**.)

B   Linking Thinking .... *Thinking Operations: Synthesis*

Study the chart of "Thinking Operations" (**542**). Focus on the box labeled "Synthesis."

CHOOSE two different courses you are taking in school right now—geometry and history, phys ed and music, etc.

FIGURE out some way of relating material from one course to material from the other.

WRITE a single clear sentence stating the relationship you see.

BROWSE through *Writers INC* and

JOT DOWN ways in which your handbook could help you expand your sentence into an essay.

C   Thinking About the Homeless .... *Thinking Operations*

Study the chart of "Thinking Operations" in *Writers INC* (**542**).

LIST the six main headings from the chart.

READ the sample argumentative research paper (**171**).

Under each of the six headings, LIST at least one detail from the paper that demonstrates that kind of thinking.

D   Dot Dot Dot .... *Using the Ellipsis*

Study the guidelines for using ellipses in the "Proofreader's Guide" (**601**).

READ the persuasive paragraph on capital punishment (**096**).

CONDENSE the capital punishment paragraph to five lines, using ellipses correctly, as if you were quoting the passage in a research paper.

(*TIP*: To help you condense the paragraph, CONSULT the instructions for writing an abstract, topic **180**.)

A ▌ Computing by Hand . . . . *Using Hand Signs*

Find the chart of "Hand Signs" and the glossary of "Computer Terms" in the appendix of *Writers INC*.

> WRITE a paragraph about how you feel when you see someone using sign language.
> CHOOSE a partner.
> USE hand signs to spell out a computer term from the glossary.
> LET your partner find the definition and read it aloud.
> REVERSE roles and do it again.
> WRITE a paragraph about how you feel personally when *you* use sign language to "speak" with your partner.

B ▌ I Was Going to Be a Writer . . . . *Using Pronouns*

Review the section on "Pronouns" in *Writers INC* (**849-868**).

> READ "I was going to be a father . . ." on the first page of *Writers INC*.
> COUNT the pronouns on this page—there are about 90 in all. How many can you find?
> WRITE your own essay speculating on "Why We Write."

C ▌ What Color Is Your Author? . . . . *Kinds of Sentences*

Study section **919** of *Writers INC*, which explains the differences between *simple, compound, complex,* and *compound-complex* sentences.

> CHOOSE two articles from a well-written modern magazine like *Harper's, Esquire, Ebony, Omni, The New Yorker, The New Republic,* or *The Atlantic Monthly.*
> CHOOSE one column of copy from one of the articles.
> LINE each sentence in the column with a colored marker, crayon, pencil, or pen.
> USE a different color for each of the four types of sentences (red for simple, blue for compound, green for complex, and yellow for compound-complex).
> REPEAT the process for the second article.
> WRITE DOWN the differences you observe between the two writers' sentences.

A ⬛ Going in Style · *Types of Sentences*

Study topic **920** in *Writers INC* to review the differences between *loose, balanced, periodic,* and *cumulative* sentences.

> CHOOSE an interesting article from a major news magazine such as *Time, Newsweek,* or *U.S. News and World Report.*
> COUNT the occurrences of each type of sentence (loose, periodic, etc.) in the article.
> DECIDE which type dominates in the writer's style.
> WRITE a comment on the article using *only* that type of sentence.
> REPEAT this process using a short chapter from one of your textbooks.

B ⬛ Everyone Must, Anyone May · · *Agreement of Subject and Verb*

Study the section in "Re-Marks" concerning "Agreement of Subject and Verb" (**921-929**).

> CHOOSE a group, club, class, council, committee, troop, or board you belong to today or have belonged to in the past.
> LIST the duties, responsibilities, options, and privileges of the group as a whole and of each of its members.
> USE as many indefinite pronouns as you can in the subject positions in your sentences.
> CHECK your sentences for subject-verb agreement in person and number.

C ⬛ Furlongs and Minims, Scruples and Drams · · · · · · · · · *Table of Weights and Measures*

In the appendix to *Writers INC*, see the "Table of Weights and Measures" (**958**).

> FIND a word in the table which you did not know before and which makes you curious.
> LOOK UP the word in a good historical dictionary such as the *Oxford English Dictionary* or a *Webster's Unabridged.*
> WRITE a brief story about the origins of the word you chose.

Level 12 Minilessons

A | Book of Wisdom .... *Using a Proverb*

Near the beginning of *Writers INC* (page 5), find the quotation, "Writing is mind traveling, destination unknown."

THINK about what this quotation means; then WRITE your own quotation about writing.

COLLECT your class's quotations and prepare a handout (or series of posters) of "Wisdom for Writers."

B | Pyramid Power .... *Prewriting*

What are the six steps in "cubing," a useful technique for prewriting? (*Tip*: Check topic **033** in *Writers INC*.)

THINK and WRITE: Make up useful instructions for a new prewriting technique called "Pyramid Power," using a four-sided pyramid as your model. What would each side of your pyramid stand for?

C | Thinking To, Thinking From .... *Inductive Reasoning*

Using the index of *Writers INC*, find and read three passages where the difference between *inductive reasoning* and *deductive reasoning* is explained.

For the brave: WRITE an *inductive* paragraph defining "inductive reasoning" and a *deductive* paragraph defining "deductive reasoning."

D | Talking Eyes .... *Evaluating Your Writing*

Read the section on being a "Three-Eyed Writer" (**115**).

CHOOSE a writing assignment you need to finish for one of your classes.

WRITE a three-way dialogue about your assignment; let the "material eye" see and say what the writing is going to be about; let the "critical eye" see and say what is good or bad about your approach; and let the "intuitive eye" see and say what the overall impact of your assignment should be.

A ∎ Getting to the Root . . . . *Building Vocabulary*

Read the guidelines for "Writing a Definition" in *Writers INC* (**122**).
> TURN to the "Dictionary of Prefixes" (**446**), "Suffixes" (**447**), and "Roots" (**448**).
> WRITE a reasonable-sounding definition for each of the following make-believe words, after consulting the "Dictionary of Prefixes, Suffixes, and Roots":
>> *amphidictive*   *micromorphosteoid*   *similcalorizoic*
>> *perfractacardiology*   *retrojectophobia*   *philidiocapticule*
>> *submatrifumalgia*   *pseudopolyacergastrorhea*   *presolidentomy*
> PUT together your own words and challenge the class to write a definition for each.

B ∎ And Then, And Then . . . . *Reworking Cliches*

Under "Writing About an Event" in *Writers INC* (**123**), read through the list of cliches and worn-out expressions to avoid.
> CHOOSE one of the cliches and
> USE the cliche in a sentence about a public event you were once part of (a wedding, a graduation, a political rally, an execution—you know).
> REWRITE the sentence with original language in place of the cliche.

C ∎ Stellar Minds . . . . *Steps in the Research Paper: Prewriting*

Turn in *Writers INC* to the chapter on "The Research Paper" and study the section "Steps in the Research Process: Prewriting" (**142-143**).
> CHOOSE one of these famous astronomers:
>> *Ptolemy*   *Copernicus*   *Galileo*
>> *Isaac Newton*   *Tycho Brahe*   *Johannes Kepler*
>> *William Herschel*   *Edmund Halley*   *Percival Lowell*
>> *Charles Messier*   *Karl Jansky*   *Carl Sagan*

> LOOK UP the astronomer you've chosen in a modern all-purpose encyclopedia or encyclopedia of astronomy.
> *NOTE* the following in the encyclopedia article, if they are available: an introductory outline, headlines, illustrations, questions for discussion, topics for cross-reference, a bibliography for further reading.
> PREPARE a preliminary bibliography on your topic.
> WRITE down a good question about your topic which your encyclopedia cannot answer.

A ▸ Card Games .... *Note Taking: A Closer Look*

Under "Steps in the Research Process" in *Writers INC*, read the section "Searching for Information" (**143**); pay special attention to "Note Taking: A Closer Look."

READ one of the featured essays at the end of a recent issue of *Time* or *Newsweek* magazine.

On one 3" x 5" note card, SUMMARIZE the whole essay.

On another card, PARAPHRASE the paragraph that best reveals the thesis of the essay.

On another card, QUOTE DIRECTLY the most memorable sentence in the essay.

On a fourth card, COMMENT PERSONALLY in response to what you've read.

B ▸ Mike Powell Holds the Long Jump Record .. *Common Knowledge in Research Papers*

Review the meaning of the phrase "common knowledge" under topic **152**.

CHOOSE your favorite subject in school—ok, phy ed and home ec included.

LIST five facts which you believe are common knowledge in that field.

ADD one fact from a published source which is not common knowledge in that field.

C ▸ Styles on Parade .... *Styles of Documenting Sources*

Three of the most common documentation styles for research papers are abbreviated MLA, APA, and CMS.

FIND OUT what these three abbreviations stand for.

LOCATE a sample of all three styles side by side, each citing a book by Marie Borroff.

LOOK very closely at every detail of the three citations and

WRITE DOWN the differences you see.

Finally, WRITE an MLA-style citation of *Writers INC*.

D ▸ Last Name, First Name .... *List of Works Cited*

Take the following bits of information and assemble them into an accurate, complete citation in a list of works cited. (Use the index to find models of MLA style for documenting sources in research papers.)

The source is a book. The book's author is Steven Levenkron. He titled his book *Treating and Overcoming Anorexia Nervosa*. The book was published in New York by Charles Scribner's Sons publishing company. It was published in 1982.

A | **Sebranek et al** . . . . *The Research Paper: Citing Books*

In the chapter on "The Research Paper,"
 SEARCH "Works Cited Entries: Books" (**157**) for the right model and
 WRITE a proper MLA-style citation for *Writers INC*.

B | **Gary Speaks** . . . . *Citing an Interview*

Suppose you were writing a research paper about homeless men under thirty years old in St. Louis who are not drug abusers, alcoholics, or mentally ill. Your research takes you out of the library into the street where you personally interview a homeless man who calls himself "Gary." You decide to use some of his comments in the introduction to your research paper.
 WRITE a citation of your interview for the "Works Cited" section of your
  research paper.
 (*TIP:* You'll find a model in *Writers INC* under "Works Cited Entries: Other
  Print and Nonprint Sources.")

C | **Amusing Ourselves to Death** . . . . *Using Quoted Material*

Read the section on "Using Quoted Material" in *Writers INC* (**153**). Especially study the instructions for handling "Partial Quotations."
 READ the following passage until you understand it:
  "Whereas television taught the magazines [like *People* and *Us*] that
  news is nothing but entertainment, the magazines have taught television
  that nothing but entertainment is news. Television programs, such as
  'Entertainment Tonight,' turn information about entertainers and celebri-
  ties into 'serious' cultural content, so that the circle begins to close: Both
  the form and content of news become entertainment."
            (Neil Postman, *Amusing Ourselves to Death,* 112)

 REWRITE the passage using ellipses (. . .) to reduce it to less than 50% of
  its original length so that only the bare essential ideas remain.
 CAUTION: In shortening the passage do not distort its meaning.

© Write Source, Box 460, Burlington, WI 53105

A | Laurel, According to Hardy .... *Parenthetical References*

Study the section on "Parenthetical References" in *Writers INC* (**154**). Focus on the instructions for citing indirect sources.

FIND an example of a *quotation from an indirect source* in the model student paper (**171**).

TAKE this information: The artist Paul Klee told his students once that "art is exactitude winged by intuition." William Zinsser quotes Klee's comment on page 55 of his book *Writing to Learn*. Zinsser says he likes Klee's comment as a definition of good writing.

WRITE a sentence about Zinsser in which you quote Klee's words, and cite them parenthetically as a quotation from an indirect source.

B | Crack That Code .... *Abbreviations in the Research Paper*

Use the index to locate a list of abbreviations for research papers.

WRITE out the words referred to by the following abbreviations:

ed., eds.	*ibid.*	*p., pp.*	*e.g.*
i.e.	*rev.*	*et al.*	*l., ll.*
rpt.	*f., ff.*	*n.d.*	*vol.*

C | Why? Why? Why? ...... *Writing to Learn: Pointed Questions*

Find the "Writing-to-Learn Activities" in *Writers INC* (**473**). Focus on activity #9, "Pointed Questions."

WRITE a sentence stating what you think would be an ideal summer job.
On the next line, WRITE the word "WHY?"
On the next line, ANSWER the question "Why" in a complete sentence.
On the next line, WRITE "WHY?" Again, answer in a complete sentence.
KEEP on going this way until you can't write anymore.
Then, REREAD what you've written and WRITE a short paragraph about what you thought about while arguing with yourself.
OR . . .If the "summer job" question leads nowhere, try this one: STATE what you would buy first if you won your state's lottery tomorrow.

D | Brainstorm .... *Right Brain/Left Brain*

Read the general description of the differences between "left brain" thinking and "right brain" thinking.

WRITE an argument about any subject between George and Martha (or Ike and Tina, or Sonny and Cher) in such a way that it is clear which one is a "right brain" thinker and which one a "left."

A Eureka! . . . . *The Short Story and the Creative Process*

Find and read "An Overview of the Creative Process" (**534**) and "The Creative Process: A Closer Look" (**535**).

RECALL a time in your own life when you had a sudden inspiration or bright idea.

INVESTIGATE the ideas and experiences that prepared you for inspiration.

WRITE an autobiographical short story in which your moment of inspiration appears *either* at the opening *or* at the climax.

B Countdown to Insanity . . *The Creative Process: First Stirrings*

Read "An Overview of the Creative Process" (**534**). Focus on the comments about "first stirrings."

SHUT your eyes, concentrate deeply, and in your mind begin slowly counting backward from one million. (While counting, don't mumble or move your lips.)

STOP when an idea other than a number creeps into your mind as you are counting.

EXPRESS your thought on paper, developing it further if you can.

RESUME counting, stopping, writing, counting, etc., until you can't stand it anymore.

C Something New
Under the Sun . . . . *The Creative Process: A Closer Look*

Find and read topic **535** in *Writers INC*, "The Creative Process: A Closer Look."

With your teacher's permission, LEAVE the classroom for 8-10 minutes with a pad of paper and pen or pencil.

Within 100 yards of your classroom, SEARCH very carefully until you discover something you're sure no other human being has ever noticed before in the history of the world.

WRITE a paragraph describing what you've seen.

In your paragraph, USE and UNDERLINE at least one of each of the following kinds of phrases:

gerund	*infinitive*	*participial*
prepositional	*appositive*	*absolute*

(FIND explanations and examples of these phrases in sections **912-915** .)

© Write Source, Box 460, Burlington, WI 53105

A ▏ Thinking About Thinking . . . . *Rational Thinking*

Read the short introduction to "Rational Thinking" (**539**), including the sections on "Metacognition" and "Cognition."

TRY to solve one of these two puzzles:

Easy: Arrange two dots and a line so that the line passes *between* the two dots even though both are on the same side of it.

Harder: Arrange six straight lines of any length so that together they form exactly 16 triangles.

When you're finished, THINK about how you *monitored* your own thinking as you struggled to solve the puzzles.

WRITE DOWN the things you remember telling (or asking) yourself.

ARRANGE your written comments in three vertical columns:

       1) How I chose my approach

       2) How I kept going

       3) How I evaluated my progress

B ▏ Constitutional Conclusions . . . . *Using Premises*

Study the definition and structure of syllogisms in "Syllogisms: The Deductive Argument" (**543**).

TURN to the list of "Amendments to the Constitution of the United States" (**963**).

CHOOSE one of the amendments which you understand and can connect with modern American life.

WRITE down the amendment as the "major" premise in a syllogism.

WRITE an appropriate statement about a specific person or situation as the "minor" premise.

COMPOSE a sentence which draws a natural conclusion from the major and minor premises.

C ▏ Buried Arguments . . . . . . *Syllogisms: The Deductive Argument*

Read topic **543** in *Writers INC*, "Syllogisms: The Deductive Argument." Focus on the definition and example of "enthymeme."

CHOOSE a partner and for a few minutes discuss whether it should be legal to burn the American flag.

LISTEN to the logic of your partner's argument.

WRITE down anything your partner says in the form of an enthymeme and discuss with him or her which logical step is taken for granted in it.

A What's It All About? . . . . *Thinking Inductively*

Read the introduction to the chapter on "Thinking Logically." Focus on the first paragraph, which explains the nature of an "inductive argument."

LOOK carefully at many different features of *Writers INC*: color, table of contents, epigraphs, headlines, charts, illustrations, guidelines, writing samples, proofreader's guide, appendices, etc.

USE inductive reasoning to draw your own conclusions about what kind of purpose *Writers INC* is meant to serve.

WRITE down your conclusions.

After you have written your conclusions, COMPARE them to the statements made in the preface, "Using the Handbook" (page *iii*).

B Weak Links . . . . *Developing a Formal Argument*

Study the "Stages of the Formal Argument" (**544**).

CHOOSE a side over one of these simple statements: 1) children should be seen and not heard, 2) guns should be allowed in the home, or 3) "no shoes, no shirt, no service."

FOLLOW the stages of argument highlighted in blue in topic **544**, jotting down notes you could use if you wrote a full argumentative essay.

REVIEW your notes and decide what is the weakest link in the chain of your argument.

DESCRIBE your conclusions to a partner.

C What Makes You Say So? . . . *The Formal Argument: Warrants*

Study the "Key Stages in the Formal Argument" (**545-551**). Focus on topic **547**, "Support," and **549**, "Warrant."

THINK of the last time you had a disagreement with a parent or supervisor.

WRITE DOWN either your *claim* or the other person's.

WRITE DOWN the key statements that were made to *support* the claim.

WRITE DOWN the *warrants* for the supporting statements.

D Give Me a Break . . . . *The Formal Argument: Concessions*

Read the "Key Stages in the Formal Argument" (**545**); focus on the section on "Concession" (**550**).

THINK of a law or rule that you think is too restrictive for people your age.

WRITE a statement arguing for a change.

Try to GUESS what arguments an opponent would use to defeat yours.

WRITE a list of *concessions* you could make to your opponent; USE several of the expressions listed in the box in topic **550**.

© Write Source, Box 460, Burlington, WI 53105

A | Coke Can Found in Mummy Case .... *Using Evidence & Logic*

Study the section on "Using Evidence and Logic" (**552-557**), especially the "Fallacies of Thinking."

BUY a copy of a tabloid-style newspaper at a supermarket checkout lane.

FIND an article or advertisement in the paper which you find *unconvincing*.

EXAMINE the logic used to sell the product or prove a point.

POINT OUT to a partner any fallacies of thinking you detect.

EXPLAIN what makes the logic false.

B | Firm/Obstinate/Pigheaded .... *Slanted Language*

In the section on "Fallacies of Thinking," focus on #19, "Slanted Language" (**556**).

RECALL the plot of a movie you've seen lately.

TELL the plot in one short paragraph in such a way that you communicate neither positive nor negative feelings about the movie.

RETELL the plot in language with a strong negative charge, as if you despised the movie.

RETELL the plot in a highly positive way, as if you loved the movie.

UNDERLINE the words that show emotional bias.

(*TIP*: Use a thesaurus to find more emotionally loaded words; see topic **201**.)

C | Who Got the OK? .... *Punctuation Review*

Scan the rules for commas (**605-619**), semicolons (**620-623**), and quotation marks (**649-657**).

TRY to punctuate the following sentence so that it makes perfect sense, using 2 commas, 1 semicolon, and 6 sets of quotation marks:

John where Jim had used just had had used had had had had had had the teacher's approval.

D | Chicken Scratchings .... *Improving Handwriting*

Study the "Handwriting Models" on the inside back cover of *Writers INC*.

COMPARE the model handwriting to a sample of your own penmanship today.

WRITE a quick and free reflection on the way your own handwriting has changed since you were first taught to write. (*How* has it changed? *Why* does handwriting change? How do you feel about it? How will it change in the future and why?)

The *Writers File:* A 9-12 Writing Program

What is the *Writers File* and how does it work?

The *File* is a complete writing series for grades 9-12 consisting of eight basic parts: a student-centered framework of writing activities, a collection of writing workshops, a variety of language and learning minilessons, a resource folder of writing prompts and management forms, a set of helpful studying and learning strategies, and a series of practical writing activities. Also included are guidelines for assessing and monitoring writing and for using the program across the curriculum. The heart of the *File* is the writing framework of 18 "sequential" writing activities for each grade level. These activities offer students a wide variety of valuable, real-life writing experiences.

How are the writing activities arranged within the framework?

The activities generally move from personal to public forms and from simple to complex structures. Each activity builds in some way on the previous writing experiences, providing students with a growing number of useful composing skills and strategies. The activities are arranged into five categories within the framework according to the kind of thinking and gathering that is required of the student. The framework should serve as a general guide, not a hard-and-fast sequence. It will give you and your students the big picture, a frame of reference when planning and implementing your individual writing program.

How are the individual writing activities presented?

Each framework activity contains three basic parts: teacher's notes, writing guidelines, and student and professional models. The guidelines and models can be reproduced or made into overhead transparencies. *Note:* Generally speaking, there are three models included for each framework activity, two student models and one professional model.

Special Note: On pp. 133-138 in this teacher's guide, you will find one complete framework activity, including the teacher's notes, student

guidelines, and writing models. (This activity comes from level 9 in the *Writers File*.)

What other activities are included in the *File?*

Writing Workshops . . . The *File* contains writing workshops with approximately 40 activities per level designed to introduce or reinforce essential prewriting, revising, editing, and proofreading strategies.

Language and Learning Activities . . . The *File* also contains a variety of language and learning activities covering everything from free writing to modeling.
- MUG Shot Sentences for increasing language awareness
- Writing Topics for gaining fluency through daily writing
- Show-Me Sentences for improving proficiency in adding details to writing
- Sentence Modeling for developing sentence-combining and styling strategies

Resource Folder . . . The resource folder contains a variety of writing prompts and management forms ready for immediate use.

Study and Learning Strategies . . . The *File* also contains a "sequence" of study and learning activities covering such topics as test taking, note taking, and using the library.

Practical Writing . . . Everything from basic paragraphs (level 9) to writing résumés (level 12) is included in these practical, on-the-job writing activities.

Writing Across the Curriculum . . . The information and activities on writing across the curriculum are the perfect complement to any schoolwide writing program.

Assessing and Monitoring . . . This section of The *File* contains guidelines, checklists, and forms for assessing and monitoring student progress.

9	10	11	12
PERSONAL WRITING			
Personal Reminiscence	Reminiscence of a Person	Reminiscence of School Life	Extended Reminiscence
Related Reminiscences	"Unpeopled" Reminiscence	Reminiscence of a Group	Personal Essay
SUBJECT WRITING			
Description of a Person	Description of a Place	Character Profile	Historical Profile
Secondhand Story	Firsthand Experience	Extended Experience	Personal Research Project
Eyewitness Account	Interview Report	Observation Report	Venture Report
Report from Single Source	Compiled Report from Multiple Interviews	Compiled Report from Multiple Sources	Group or Collaborative Report
CREATIVE WRITING			
Fictionalized Journal Entry	Fictionalized Memory	Fiction from Fact	Fictionalized Imitation
Character Sketch	Patterned Fiction	Uncharted Fiction	Genre Writing
Memory Poem	Patterned Poetry	Found/List Poetry	Statement thru Poetry
Dialogue	Monologue	Ad Script	Play Writing
REFLECTIVE WRITING			
Essay of Illustration	Essay of Explanation	Essay of Experience	Essay of Reflection
Dialogue of Ideas	Essay of Opposing Ideas	Satiric Essay	Essay of Speculation
Response to Reading	Personal Review	Limited Literary Analysis	Extended Analysis
Pet Peeve	Editorial	Commentary	Position Paper
ACADEMIC WRITING			
Essay of Information	Essay to Compare	Essay of Definition	Problem/Sol. Essay
Essay to Explain a Process	Cause/Effect Essay	Essay of Argumentation	Essay of Evaluation
*Paragraph Writing	*The Essay Test	*On-the-Job Writing	Impromptu Essay
*The Summary	*The Précis	*The Paraphrase	*The Abstract

✱ These framework activities can be found in the "Practical Writing" and "Study and Learning Strategies" sections of the *Writers File*.

A Closer Look at the Writing Framework

Each activity in the writing framework is arranged into one of five categories. The categories progress from personal to public (academic) writing, building a variety of skills and strategies along the way. Guidelines and student models are provided for each activity.

PERSONAL WRITING: *REMEMBERING & SHARING*

Students will write memory pieces from a number of different points of view. They will be asked to reminisce about their own experiences, other people, groups, school life, and so on. In the final memory piece, students will develop an extended reminiscence in which they explore a past phase (extended period of time) in their lives. The focus in this section is looking back into the past.

SUBJECT WRITING: *SEARCHING & REPORTING*

Once students have become familiar and comfortable with writing about themselves and others from memories, they will move to writing which focuses on collecting information about more public subjects. Students will be asked to write descriptions, reports, profiles, eyewitness accounts, and experience papers much like a professional feature writer. During this process they will practice observing, interviewing, researching, focusing, and compiling information. The focus here is looking into and reporting on subjects that are of current interest to the students.

CREATIVE WRITING: *INVENTING & IMITATING*

Students will also be given ample opportunities to create dialogue, stories, poems, and scripts, beginning with a fictionalized journal entry and ending with a one-act play. In the process, they will experience a wide variety of forms and strategies useful in other areas of writing. The focus here is inventing, taking memories and experiences and reshaping them into creative pieces.

REFLECTIVE WRITING: *REFLECTING & SPECULATING*

Students will next have the opportunity to utilize the strategies employed during personal, subject, and creative writing to bring their ideas, feelings, and memories together in a variety of reflective forms. Students will begin in ninth grade with a basic essay in which a story illustrates a point and end in twelfth grade with a fairly complex "position paper." The focus here is developing reflective essays in a variety of contexts.

ACADEMIC WRITING: *INFORMING & ANALYZING*

Even though any of the writing activities in the framework can be used throughout the curriculum, those in the academic category are probably used most often. Again, the range is wide—from a basic essay of information to a more challenging essay of evaluation. Students will be given opportunities to interpret, define, compare and contrast, argue, analyze, propose solutions, consider cause and effect, and evaluate. In addition, students will encounter the more traditional forms for "showing learning," among them the essay test and the different forms of summary writing. The focus here is shaping informed, coherent, and clear essays of information.

Personal Reminiscence

Teacher's Notes:

From the Beginning . . .

Discussion: When writing about a personal reminiscence, students should always keep in mind that the focus of their writing is the incident itself more than their reaction to it. Encourage students to try to *show* the incident in process using specific details, dialogue, and action words rather than *tell* their readers what happened. Effective personal writing has a sense of immediacy to it, an as-it-happened quality from start to finish. Remind students that they will be engaged in a type of narrative writing in this activity *(First this happened . . . Then I went . . . After . . .).*

Students should ask the following types of questions as they shape their writing:

❑ What is there about my subject that will make it interesting and/or entertaining?

❑ Do I know all of the basic information related to the incident? *(Who? What? When? Where? Why? How?)*

❑ Should I start right in the middle of the action or provide some background information first?

❑ What specific details will help bring the incident to life for my readers?

❑ What tone or feeling do I want my writing to project? *(Serious? Humorous? Silly? Sarcastic? Sad?)*

Special Note: It's important that students put some distance between themselves and their subjects since the intention of this activity is to have students draw from their memories, not from their immediate experiences.

Additional Selecting Activity: If students are having trouble selecting a subject, have them write freely (or list ideas) about a particular period or aspect in their lives (summers in an old neighborhood, holidays, vacations, illnesses, former friends, etc.) to see what possible writing ideas they can generate.

Thinking Operations Related to the Personal Reminiscence:

Certainly *recalling* and *selecting* are the two most important thinking operations students will employ in this activity. In addition, they will have to carefully assess and organize the facts and details they have gathered and perhaps do a bit of creative thinking to fill in the gaps or create a sense of the experience rather than provide a literal play-by-play commentary.

Quotation for Discussion:

> *"A writer's material is what he cares about."*
> —John Gardner

Related Workshops:

"Creating a Plan of Action," p. 15
"Where the Sidewalk Ends, p. 12

Focused Assignment Option:

Assignment: Share a personal memory related to a frightening experience.

Subject: Think of incidents in your life that have caused your heart to skip a few beats.)

Purpose: To share and entertain

Audience: Classmates

Form: Personal writing

Voice: Familiar or informal

Cross-Curricular Applications:

● Share a memory that helped you better understand the workings of nature, the workings of science, etc. (Science)

● Share a memory related to an aspect of technology—building something, solving a problem, etc. (Tech-Prep)

● Share a memory related to living in a city or the country, personal relationships, etc. (Social Studies, Family Living)

● Take on the role of a historical figure and share a personal experience. (History)

From the Beginning . . .

*Discussion: Share an unforgettable incident or event from your past that happened over a relatively short period of time. This incident might have taken only a few minutes, or perhaps it extended over a few hours or the better part of a day. You might focus on a thrilling adventure, a silly incident, a serious or solemn event, a frightening few minutes . . . Be sure to include enough specific detail to make your writing come alive for your readers. Provided below are basic guidelines to help you develop your work. Also note the models following these guidelines. Additional information can be found in the handbook. (Refer to "*WRITING*, About an event" in the index.)*

▶ *Searching and Selecting*

1. **SELECTING**   You should have little trouble thinking of a subject to write about. You're simply looking for an incident that appeals to you personally and that will have some appeal to your readers.

2. **REVIEWING**   Review your journal entries for ideas for your writing. Or focus your attention on a specific time in your past and list related ideas as they come to mind. Then again you might want to talk about the good old days with a friend or classmate.

   Special Note: If the subject of your writing is vivid in your memory, go right to the first draft if you want. Otherwise, follow the guidelines for "Generating the Text."

▶ *Generating the Text*

3. **RECORDING**   Write freely about your subject, once you have one in mind, to see how much you already know about it and what you need to find out. (Try writing nonstop for at least five minutes.)

4. **COLLECTING**   Collect additional details if necessary, using the suggestions in the handbook as your guide. (Refer to "Writing About an Event" for these suggestions.)

5. **FOCUSING**   State a possible focus or idea you want to express in your writing. Then plan accordingly, selecting and organizing details that support this impression.

▶ *Writing and Revising*

6. **WRITING**   Write your first draft freely, working in details as they naturally come to mind or according to your planning.

7. **REVISING**   Carefully review, revise, and refine your writing before sharing it. Remember that your goal is to re-create this incident in living color for your readers. (Refer to "Final Re-Marks" when you are ready to proofread your work.)

▶ *Evaluating*

- Is the writing focused around a specific incident or event?
- Does the writing contain effective supporting details?
- Does the writing sound sincere and honest?
- Will readers appreciate the treatment of this subject?

Adventure and excitement often come in strange shapes and sizes for children. In the following model, writer Rod Vick recalls the time he learned how to sled in the summer—on a block of ice, no less. Maybe you have a thrill-seeking adventure of your own to share? Read "Ice Blocking" and see how it can be done.

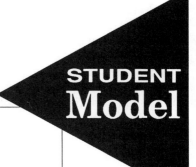

ICE Blocking

I always thought it was impossible to go sledding without snow. But that was before I tried "ice blocking" one warm summer day a few years ago. Some friends, who were experienced in the sport, and I bought six 10-pound blocks of ice from a local gas station. Then we wheeled the heavy blocks in some wagons to the top of a large, grassy hill in a nearby park. I remember the hill being much steeper than I had at first thought. I watched in amazement as my friends held each block in place while the rider laid a towel over the ice before mounting. As soon as the holder let go, the rider was off, moving slowly at first, but quickly picking up speed as the ice began to melt from the friction. One by one, my friends took their turns—slip-sliding their way down the hill. The hill soon turned into a gooey mess which made getting the ice block up the hill seem almost as challenging as the ride down.

It all looked like too much fun to resist, so finally I gathered up the courage to try. It wasn't easy sitting on the ice, but that was nothing compared to controlling the slippery sled as it shot full bore down a hill. I hadn't realized that a block of ice could go so fast and in a path almost entirely of its own making. Near the bottom of my first ride, I hit a major bump and flew off, rolling over and over in the muck. When I came to a stop, I was coated with mud and grass and lucky not to have broken a leg or an arm or something else in the process.

The fundamentals of ice blocking are described in the opening paragraph.

The details of the author's first ride are relived in the second paragraph.

In this model, writer Laura Baginski shares an entertaining incident involving herself (obviously), her mother, and a tomato. Pay special attention to Ms. Baginski's attitude throughout the piece. Does she seem to set herself up for the surprising finish? (This model appeared in the June 1992 commemorative issue of *The High School Writer,* a monthly publication of student writing. It is reprinted with permission.)

Tomato on the Brain

"If you keep crossing your eyes like that, young lady, they'll stay like that and you won't ever get married." My mother was at it again. She went on to say, "It's true. There was a little girl in Bolivia who crossed her eyes just like you do and then it was permanent. She died all alone." Words of wisdom from my all-knowing mother. She seemed to have a lethal warning or terrifying story about anything that gave me the slightest bit of pleasure. "If you keep eating candy like that, your teeth will fall out and then you'll look like those disgusting hillbillies you see on TV."

I never listened to her. I would sit there with my eyes crossed, shoveling chocolate into my mouth just to show her. Defying my mother was a kind of mission for me. She knew this, and it terrified her all the more.

One day I was hanging upside down from my knees on my monkey bars. I glanced around the yard. Hanging there, the world was completely rearranged; the trees looked like feather dusters, the basket of vegetables underneath me seemed to replace the clouds, and my dog seemed to be flying. My mother was laboriously caring for her precious yet weed-infested garden. She worked in such jerking, hummingbird-like movements that watching her from an upside-down position was a special and amusing treat.

Wiping sweat off her brow, she peered at me over her shoulder and shook her head. "You know, if you hang upside down like that, all the blood rushing to your brain will make your head blow up."

I smiled. A challenge. This was what I had been waiting for. The sheer excitement of the possibility of my head exploding motivated me to hang there longer.

After five minutes, my temples began to throb. My heart felt like a big lump of pain and seemed to weigh at least 200 pounds. My entire body was numb. I could feel all the blood rushing to my brain like a flash flood. My mother's wise warnings jabbed and replayed over and over in my mind. I was suddenly gripped with the realization that my head was indeed going to blow up.

I tried to get down, but paralysis seized me. In a panic, I closed my eyes and envisioned fragments of my head strewn around the yard. I saw myself transformed into fertilizer for my mother's garden, my severed eyes and nose in my father's tomato patch, dripping off the lilac patch, flowing down the fence. . . .

Suddenly, darkness washed over me and I was falling, sinking . . . until my head struck something offering little resistance. The impact jolted me out of my trance.

As my eyes tried to focus, I reached my hand to my head, checking to see how much of it was left. What my hand discovered was soft, mushy, brainlike. Struck with terror, I brought my trembling hand to my focusing eyes. It was oozing, it was red, it was . . . it was . . . a tomato!

Specific examples of her mother's words of wisdom are provided.

The main focus of the writing is the monkey-bars affair.

The writer goes to "extremes" in describing her dangerous situation.

The drama increases until the messy end of the incident.

STUDENT
Model

My mind went blank . . .

Most of my first 15 years have been pretty typical, but there is one experience that sticks out above all the others. It changed my life forever.

I was around nine years old and my sisters were ten and seven, and not one of us was old enough to understand what was going on. All we knew was that Dad worked second shift, and that he was rarely home on weekends. While he was at work, my mother would go out, so we really didn't see either of them together very much. When we did, they would do nothing but holler at each other. As one would expect, this was upsetting to children our age, so we often ran to our rooms and pretended not to hear.

As I remember it now, it was a Monday, a day they must have been planning for a long time. My sisters and I had just come home from school, and my dad was waiting inside the door. But he didn't even say hello when we came in. He just said, "As soon as you take off your school clothes, your mother and I would like to talk to you in the front room." We knew something was wrong because my father was home in the middle of the afternoon, and his voice was stern when he spoke to us. We could also see that my mother had been crying.

We changed quickly and quietly, without the usual sisterly squabbling. We were soon in the front room, wrapped around our mother, trying our best to comfort each other. My dad began to talk. "Girls, from now on, I'm going to be home when you get home from school." For a moment I was relieved. Then, he finished, "There will be one other change—your mother will not be living with us any longer." The smile fell from my face. My mind went blank, and I must have gone into a mild case of shock. I remember seeing my sisters crying hysterically, but I couldn't cry. I just stared at my dad. I knew he was talking again, but I couldn't hear what he was saying.

I saw my mother get up and walk toward the door. She had a suitcase in her hand, and my sisters were walking with her. She stopped and gave them a big hug and kiss. But I just stood there and stared. I couldn't kiss her good-bye—I just stood there frozen. I knew she was talking to me, but I couldn't hear anything. I did hear the door close and, like a robot, I walked to the front window. Then as my mother pulled away, the spell was broken, and I began to cry. From then on all I did was cry and wonder why this was happening to me.

In the days and weeks ahead, I slowly adjusted to our new life. I began to realize why certain things happen, why a husband and wife sometimes have to go their separate ways—even when there are children involved. I came to realize that they weren't doing this for strictly selfish reasons, and they certainly didn't want to hurt their children. They knew that continuing to live together would only bring more problems and more hurt to everyone involved. I love them both for all they've done for me and my sisters. Still, I hope my children never have to live through a similar experience. ■

A dramatic opening immediately grabs the reader's attention.

The writer focuses her attention on the specific incident as it happened.

A dramatic interchange between the mother and daughter is recalled in great detail.

The writer puts the experience into perspective for herself and her readers.

Professional
Model

Tarantulas

"Turn out, boys—the tarantulas is loose!"

No warning ever sounded so dreadful. Nobody tried, any longer, to leave the room, lest he might step on a tarantula. Every man groped [reached] for a trunk or a bed, and jumped on it. Then followed the strangest silence—a silence of grisly suspense it was, too—waiting, expectancy, fear. It was as dark as pitch, and one had to imagine the spectacle of those fourteen scant-clad men roosting gingerly on trunks and beds, for not a thing could be seen. Then came occasional little interruptions of the silence, and one could recognize a man and tell his locality by his voice, or locate any other sound a sufferer made by his gropings or changes of position. The occasional voices were not given to much speaking—you simply heard a gentle ejaculation of "Ow!" followed by a solid thump, and you knew the gentleman had felt a hairy blanket or something touch his bare skin and had skipped from a bed to the floor. Another silence. Presently you would hear a gasping voice say:

"Su-su-something's crawling up the back of my neck!"

Every now and then you could hear a little subdued scramble and a sorrowful "O Lord!" and then you knew that somebody was getting away from something he took for a tarantula, and not losing any time about it, either. Directly a voice in the corner rang out wild and clear: "I've got him! I've got him!" [Pause, and probable change of circumstances.] "No, he's got me! Oh, ain't they never going to fetch a lantern . . . !"

The landscape presented when the lantern flashed into the room was picturesque, and might have been funny to some people, but not to us. Although we were perched so strangely upon boxes, trunks, and beds, and so strangely attired, too, we were too earnestly distressed [upset] and too genuinely miserable to see any fun about it, and there was not the semblance of a smile anywhere here visible. I know I am not capable of suffering more than I did during those few minutes of suspense in the dark, surrounded by those creeping, bloody-minded tarantulas. I had skipped from bed to bed and from box to box in a cold agony, and every time I touched anything that was furzy I fancied I felt the fangs. I had rather go to war than live that episode over again.

A sense of drama and "danger" are established in the first main paragraph.

Presenting the spoken words of some of the men adds realism to the writing.

Take special note of the words Twain uses. What "landscape" is he talking about? What does he mean by "furzy"?

Writing Workshops

Searching and Selecting Topics

Understanding the Process

Selecting Interesting Subjects

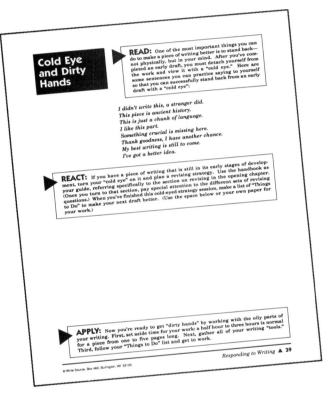

Cold Eye and Dirty Hands

READ: One of the most important things you can do to make a piece of writing better is to stand back—not physically, but in your mind. After you've completed an early draft, you must detach yourself from the work and view it with a "cold eye." Here are some sentences you can practice saying to yourself so that you can successfully stand back from an early draft with a "cold eye":

I didn't write this, a stranger did.
This piece is ancient history.
This is just a chunk of language.
I like this part.
Something crucial is missing here.
Thank goodness, I have another chance.
My best writing is still to come.
I've got a better idea.

REACT: If you have a piece of writing that is still in its early stages of development, turn your "cold eye" on it and plan a revising strategy. Use the handbook as your guide, referring specifically to the section on revising in the opening chapter. (Once you turn to that section, pay special attention to the different sets of revising questions.) When you've finished this cold-eyed strategy session, make a list of "Things to Do" to make your next draft better. (Use the space below or your own paper for your work.)

APPLY: Now you're ready to get "dirty hands" by working with the oily parts of your writing. First, set aside time for your work: a half hour to three hours is normal for a piece from one to five pages long. Next, gather all of your writing "tools." Third, follow your "Things to Do" list and get to work.

Responding to Writing ▲ 39

© Write Source, Box 460, Burlington, WI 53105

The Essentials of Life

When I was in school, I always hated it when my English teacher told me I could write on anything I wanted. Actually, I could write pretty well as long as I had something to write about, but I hated picking the subject. It just seemed as if the world was too full of things to write about, and none of them seemed right.

But, of course, there are ways of picking out and narrowing down a subject for a personal essay (and any other kind of writing for that matter). I just didn't know any at the time. In the activity which follows, I'll show you one.

REACT: Open your handbook to "Guidelines for Selecting a Subject." (Look in the handbook index under "SELECTING a subject" to locate this information.) First read about clustering and study the diagram. Then find the "Essentials of Life Checklist" and plunk your finger down anywhere on that list. Check to see which of life's essentials you landed on and write that word in the circle below; then cluster for ideas related to that category.

WRITE: On your own paper, write as quickly and freely as you can for 5 minutes on whatever subject emerged from your clustering. Then, in small groups, discuss your subjects. Talk out your ideas. Is your subject narrow enough? What about gathering information? Do you think you will be able to gather everything you need to write about this subject? Use this checklist-clustering-listing-talking exercise the next time you don't know what to write about.

© Write Source, Box 460, Burlington, WI 53105
Selecting Interesting Subjects ▲ 9

Reviewing and Revising Texts

Advising in Peer Groups

Reviewing Paragraphs & Essays

Applying Revising Strategies

Reshaping Context

Refining: Sentence Strengthening

Combining Sentences

Building Sentences

Focusing on Style

Double Whammy

Most sentences contain several basic ideas which work together to form a complete thought. For example, if you were to write a sentence about a power failure that struck your school (don't you wish!) causing a number of problems, you might be working with at least six different ideas. Each of these ideas could be written as a separate sentence.

1. There was a power failure.
2. The power failure hit the school.
3. The power failure hit without warning.
4. The failure left the lower-level classes completely in the dark.
5. The failure left the tech-ed classes without operable equipment.
6. The failure left the cafeteria staff with a pile of half-cooked hot dogs.

REVIEW: An experienced writer can use a number of methods to combine all of these ideas into longer, smoother-reading sentences. Carefully review "Guidelines for Combining Sentences" in the handbook for explanations and examples of 10 basic methods of combining. (Refer to "SENTENCE combining" in the index to find this information.) You may already use many of these methods naturally and effortlessly in your own writing; the others will become part of your toolbox of writing skills with time and practice.

APPLY: Combine the information in sentences one through six above in the four different ways indicated below. (Refer to the section on sentence combining in the handbook for models.) You do not have to include all of the information in your combined sentences. Also add or change words as necessary.

1. (Use a series to combine three or more similar ideas.)

2. (Use a relative pronoun—*who, whose, that, which*—to introduce a less important idea.)

3. (Use an introductory phrase or clause for the less important idea.)

4. (Use a participial phrase—*ing* or *ed* phrase—at the beginning or end of a sentence.)

© Write Source, Box 460, Burlington, WI 53105
Combining Sentences ▲ 49

Refining: Working with Words

Focusing on Word Choice

Working with Verb Tenses

Generating and Developing Texts

Limiting Your Subject

Searching and Shaping Subjects

Organizing Writing

Working with Ideas

Painting Pictures

Writing is the process of transferring what is in your mind to your reader's mind. Suppose in your mind you see a majestic moose, with head held high, crashing out of a forest of tall pine trees.

Now suppose you write, "The animal came out of the woods." How clearly do you think you would have communicated your original thought, or image, to the reader? Obviously, not very clearly. By using **specific words**, you can create a **specific word picture** for your reader.

Look at the examples below. Notice that the nouns move from very general at the top to very specific at the bottom. By using **specific nouns** in your writing, you will make it easier for the reader to "see" the picture you have in your mind.

person	place	thing	idea
man	park	instrument	feeling
politician	national park	musical instrument	good feeling
Abraham Lincoln	Yosemite Nat. Park	electric guitar	love

▶ **SPECIFY:** Now think of three nouns for each of the categories below. Each word you add must be more specific than the one before (as in the example above).

person	place	thing	idea

Create a clearer picture

Turn Telling into Showing

If your writing just hangs there, lifeless, maybe that's because you're telling too much and showing too little. Lovely writing moves the way a hummingbird moves: it darts in to suck up the sweet details and then backs up to look things over. If you spend all of your time looking things over, you and your reader will go hungry.

(See "Showing versus Telling" in your handbook for three examples of the way showing can give life to bland telling statements.)

▶ **READ:** Here's a telling statement that may sound fairly interesting as it stands:

Roy's mother and father tended his knife wound in a way that showed how deeply they were suffering.

However, this sentence simply tells the reader what to think rather than leading a reader through the thought by showing details. Here is how the acclaimed African-American writer James Baldwin *showed* the idea in *Go Tell It on the Mountain:* (To fully appreciate this paragraph, listen to it read out loud, and read it out loud yourself.)

His father and mother, a small basin of water between them, knelt by the sofa where Roy lay, and his father was washing the blood from Roy's forehead. It seemed that his mother, whose touch was so much more gentle, had been thrust aside by his father, who could not bear to have anyone else touch his wounded son. And now she watched, one hand in the water, the other in a kind of anguish, at her waist. . . . Her face, as she watched, was full of pain and fear, of tension basely supported, and of pity that could scarcely have been expressed had she filled all the world with her weeping. His father muttered sweet, delirious things to Roy, and his hands, when he dipped them again in the basin and wrung out the cloth, were trembling.

▶ **REFLECT:** How do you "show" in writing? Think in terms of the 5W's and H (who? what? when? where? why? and how?). Make sure that your writing answers these questions. Also think in terms of the three different types of details: sensory, memory, and reflective. Refer to "DETAILS" in the index of your handbook.

▶ **WRITE:** Here are three sentences that tell rather than show. Raise at least one of ... a paragraph full of detail. (If none of these sen...

Ideas ▲ 23

Keep It Clear

When you edit your writing, examine each sentence for incomplete comparisons, mixed construction, nonstandard language, shift in construction, and double negatives. Each of these writing errors causes problems with clarity and weakens your writing.

▶ **REACT & REWRITE:** Each of the following sentences contains one of the writing errors just mentioned. Underline the error and identify it in the space provided. Then rewrite the sentences and correct the problem. Refer to "SENTENCE, Writing effectively" in your handbook index if you need help.

1. Reading a detective novel is better. *(incomplete comparison) Reading a detective novel is better than watching reruns of The Brady Bunch.*

2. My teacher told the class that she doesn't have no patience for goof-offs and bullies.

3. When a child wants a pet, they must be willing to care for it.

4. Marvel and me got away with the cherry bomb escapade, but Rich got caught.

5. I was going to start in on the dishes right after *L.A. Law,* but my mom yelled at me anyways.

6. A kazoo is when you have a wood or metal whistle that you hum into to make music.

▶ **WRITE:** Write one long sentence that contains three of these errors. Then challenge a classmate to a search-and-destroy mission: give the person 5 minutes to find and fix all three. If your partner succeeds, shake his/her hand and say, "Hey, you done good, Dude!" (nonstandard language)

68 ▲ *Editing for Clarity*

© Write Source, Box 460, Burlington, WI 53105

Test Yourself

▶ **IDENTIFY:** In the following sentences, groups of words with one or more punctuation or usage errors are underlined and numbered in parentheses. Copy the underlined words on the blank spaces making the necessary corrections as you go along. (Be careful to show the exact location of each punctuation mark.)

Plato an (1) ancient Greek philosopher and educator was (2) the first to write about the lost continent of Atlantis. Most scholars agree that Plato book (3) entitled Critias (4) includes only legendary events not (5) real history. In his book, Plato was writing about events which he claimed happened over 9000 (6) years before his own lifetime. When Plato described atlantis he (7) painted a picture of a people of fabulous wealth who ruled over a great and wonderful empire. He said the royal palace was "a marvel to behold for size and beauty. Plato (8) also claimed that the continent of Atlantis sunk beneath the sea in one days time. (9)

If Atlantis really existed where (10) was it located? Many places have been candidates for the honor however the (11) following locations are most commonly listed the (12) Atlantic Ocean the (13) Sahara Desert, the island of Crete, Spain, England, Greenland, and Mexico.

Is their lost (14) treasure waiting for someone to discover or (15) was Atlantis only the product of Plato's imagination? Wouldnt it (16) be marvelous if someone found the fabled land of gold and silver where Plato said kings gathered every five years to administer the laws hunt (17) bulls and (18) make sacrifices to the gods? Atlantis has been many things to many people but mostly (19) of all it is what it will always be (20) a mystery.

1. *Plato, an*
2. _____
3. _____
4. _____
5. _____
6. _____
7. _____
8. _____
9. _____
10. _____
11. _____
12. _____
13. _____
14. _____
15. _____
16. _____
17. _____
18. _____
19. _____
20. _____

78 ▲ *Proofreading Pretest*

© Write Source, Box 460, Burlington, WI 53105

Refining: Editing

Editing Checklist

Editing for Clarity

Editing for Sentence Errors

Refining: Proofreading

Proofreading Checklist

Proofreading for Punctuation

Proofreading for Usage

Language and Learning

MUG Shot Sentences

Writing Topics

Writing Topics

Teachers today know that students don't learn how to write by picking at various pieces of grammar or by dissecting sentences. Grammar instruction at the start of a writing program may even be a hindrance. And throwing students into a graded theme assignment can be just as shaky a beginning. We now know that the most effective way to get students into writing is simply to let them write . . . and write . . . and write . . . freely. This helps them develop a feel for writing, real writing, writing that originates from their own thoughts and feelings. It makes perfect sense to us now, but for years students were so preoccupied with "writing skills" that they never had the chance to feel comfortable with writing itself.

Implementation

No other activity gets students into writing more effectively than personal journal writing. And no other writing activity is so easy to implement. Ask any teacher who has his or her students write in journals. All students need are journals and pens, time to write (at least 10 minutes every day), and encouragement to explore whatever is on their minds. That's all it takes.

The lists of high-interest writing topics on the following pages provide your students with over 50 starting points for their personal or journal writing. The topics are organized according to type and theme to make them easier to find and use.

Once students get into a regular journal-writing routine, a number of things will take place:

- They will become interested in writing because they are allowed to write about issues and ideas important to them.

- They will begin to feel comfortable with the physical act of writing.

- They will find it easier to develop compositions because they will have so many ideas to draw from in their journals.

- They will begin to appreciate writing as a process of shaping and refining their own thinking.

- And lastly, they will put more effort into their finished products because writing will have become more personal and meaningful to them.

Note: See "Journal Writing" in the handbook for more information. Also see our catalog for personal writing journals available from the Write Source.

MUG SHOT SENTENCES ▼   Answers to page 4

■ *Abbreviation, Capitalization, Comma (Numbers)*

the average american generates 1000 lbs of recyclable garbage each year

The average American generates 1,000 pounds of recyclable garbage each year.

■ *Abbreviation, Usage (Right Word), Shift in Verb Tense*

paint accounts for about 60% of the hazardous waist that came from homes

Paint accounts for about 60 percent of the hazardous waste that comes from homes.

■ *Punctuation (Introductory Phrase), Hyphen (Single-thought Adjective), Usage (Right Word), Plurals (Spelling)*

by the year 2000 more then half the kids in America will have spent part of there lifes in single parent homes

By the year 2000, more than half the kids in America will have spent part of their lives in single-parent homes.

■ *Parentheses (To Enclose Explanatory Phrase), Usage (Right Word), Semicolon*

oceans are as much as 90 percent barren completely without life: they're like wet desserts

Oceans are as much as 90 percent barren (completely without life); they're like wet deserts.

Show-Me Sentences

Producing Writing with Detail

Teachers from time immemorial have said to their students, "Your essay lacks details and examples" or "This idea is too general" or "Show, don't tell." We've even heard of a teacher who had a special stamp made because he became so tired of writing "Give more examples" on student writing. So how should this problem be approached? It's obvious that simply telling students to add more details and examples is not enough. Even showing them how professional writers develop their ideas is not enough (although this does help). Students learn to add substance and depth to their writing through regular practice.

Here's one method that has worked for many students and teachers: Have students develop basic **Show-Me** sentences (*My locker is messy*) into brief paragraphs or essays that show rather than tell.

Model Showing Writing

My baby sister was the picture of health.
(cliche)

Josie flitted from one thing to another, as if everything in the kitchen were there for her amusement. She had already left a trail of pots, pans, bananas, and crackers behind her. Flashing Mom a bright-eyed smile, she reached her dimpled hands toward her juice cup. The juice dribbled down her chin as she drank. A swipe across her plump cheeks with her hand took care of that. She plunked the half-empty cup on the counter and started to sing to herself as she marched around the kitchen table. A sound from the yard suddenly caught her attention, and she ran toward the back door on eager, little legs.

Implementation

Before you ask students to work on their own, develop a Show-Me sentence as a class. Start by writing an example sentence on the board. Then have students volunteer specific details that give this basic thought some life. List these ideas on the board. Next, construct a brief paragraph on the board or overhead using some of these details. (Make no mention of the original sentence in your paragraph.) Discuss the results. Make sure that your students see how specific details help create a visual image for the reader. Also have your students read and react to examples of showing writing from professional texts. (Share the model above with your students.)

- Have them work on their first Show-Me sentences in class. Upon completion of their writing, have pairs of students share the results of their work. Then ask for volunteers to share their writing with the entire class. (Make copies of strong showing writing for future class discussions.)

▶ Sentences for Modeling

The main clause in each cumulative sentence is in italics.

He was up the steps and in the small vestibule in no time, pressing the bell under the card that said "Mrs. Ulgine Barrows."
—"The Catbird Seat," James Thurber

We slid the boxcar door wide open at dawn to see a vast prairie, pale gold in the east, dark in the west.
—"On Running Away," John Keats

The hotel lobby was a dark, derelict room, narrow as a corridor, and seemingly without air.
—"Total Eclipse," Annie Dillard

Soon the men began to gather, surveying their own children, speaking of planting and rain, tractors and taxes.
—"The Lottery," Shirley Jackson

The candidate swings neatly to [the] left, hands raised, two forefingers of each hand making the victory salute.
—"The Twenty-Ninth Republican Convention," Gore Vidal

A thrifty homemaker, wife, mother of three, *she also did all of her own cooking.*
—"The Little Store," Eudora Welty

An entire building had been constructed to quarantine them on their return, a species of hospital dormitory, gallery and laboratory for the moon rocks.
—"The Psychology of Astronauts," Norman Mailer

My fingers a-tremble, *I complied,* smelling the fresh leather and finding an official-looking document inside.
—*Invisible Man,* Ralph Ellison

Staring at the unblemished blue of the sky, listening to the children shout, "Rise, Sally rise, wipe your pretty eyes," *I turned that question over in my mind.*
—*The Friends,* Rosa Guy

I stand in the ghetto classroom—"the guest speaker"—attempting to lecture on the mystery of the sounds of our words to rows of diffident (hesitant) students.
—"The Achievement of Desire," Richard Rodriguez

Show-Me Sentences

Sentence Modeling and Expanding

Resource Folder

Classroom Management Forms
Mapping Frames

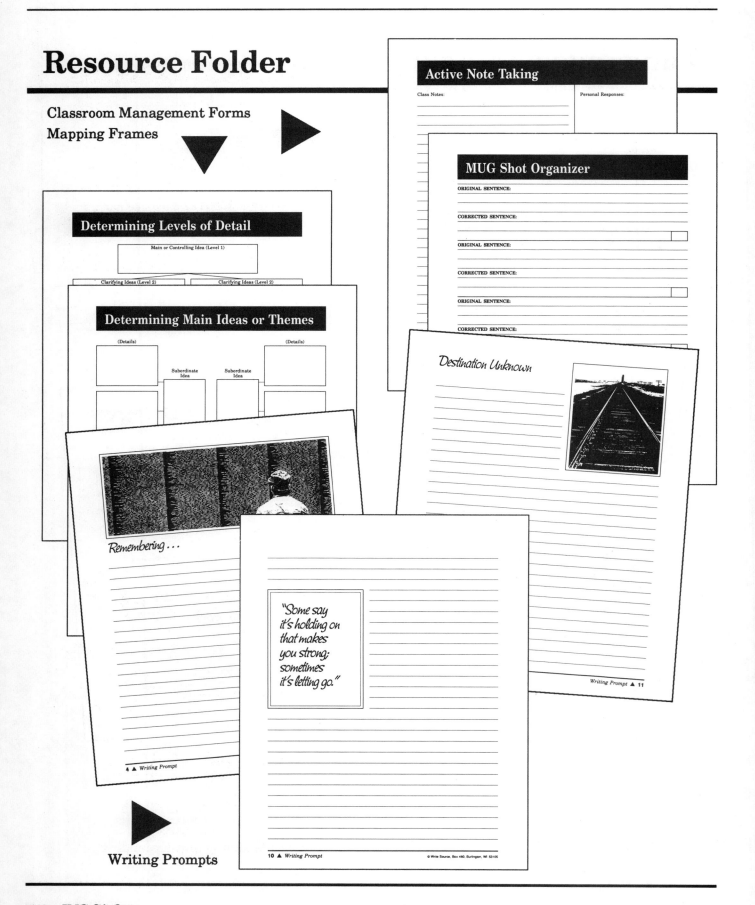

Active Note Taking

Class Notes: Personal Responses:

MUG Shot Organizer

ORIGINAL SENTENCE:

CORRECTED SENTENCE:

ORIGINAL SENTENCE:

CORRECTED SENTENCE:

ORIGINAL SENTENCE:

CORRECTED SENTENCE:

ORIGINAL SENTENCE:

CORRECTED SENTENCE:

Determining Levels of Detail

Main or Controlling Idea (Level 1)

Clarifying Ideas (Level 2)   Clarifying Ideas (Level 2)

Determining Main Ideas or Themes

(Details)   (Details)

Subordinate   Subordinate
Idea   Idea

Destination Unknown

Writing Prompt ▲ 11

Remembering . . .

4 ▲ *Writing Prompt*

*"Some say
it's holding on
that makes
you strong;
sometimes
it's letting go."*

10 ▲ *Writing Prompt*   © Write Source, Box 460, Burlington, WI 53105

Writing Prompts

Learning Strategies

Using the Library
Study-Reading Strategies
Organizing Details

9 ▼

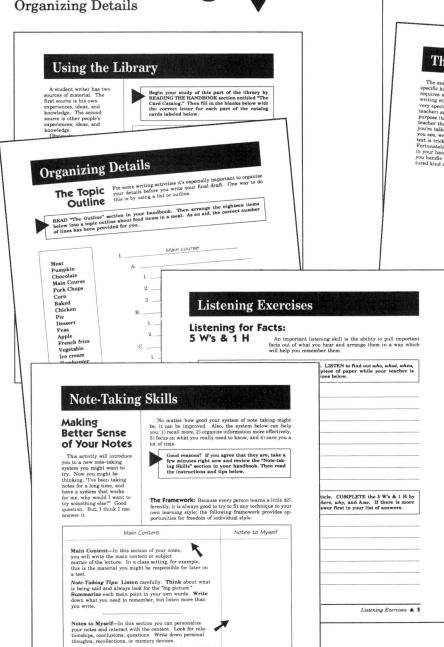

Using the Library

A student writer has two sources of material. The first source is his own experiences, ideas, and knowledge. The second source is other people's experiences, ideas, and knowledge. Obviously...

▶ Begin your study of this part of the library by READING THE HANDBOOK section entitled "The Card Catalog." Then fill in the blanks below with the correct letter for each part of the catalog cards labeled below.

Organizing Details

The Topic Outline   For some writing activities it's especially important to organize your details before you write your final draft. One way to do this is by using a list or outline.

▶ READ "The Outline" section in your handbook. Then arrange the eighteen items below into a topic outline about food items in a meal. As an aid, the correct number of lines has been provided for you.

Meat
Pumpkin
Chocolate
Main Course
Pork Chops
Corn
Baked
Chicken
Pie
Dessert
Peas
Apple
French fries
Vegetable
Ice cream
Hamburger

I. _____ Main course
  A. _____
    1. _____
    2. _____
    3. _____
  B. _____
    1. _____
    2. _____
  C. _____
    1. _____

Listening Exercises

Listening for Facts: 5 W's & 1 H

An important listening skill is the ability to pull important facts out of what you hear and arrange them in a way which will help you remember them.

..., LISTEN to find out *who, what, when,* ... piece of paper while your teacher is ... lines below.

... ticle. COMPLETE the 5 W's & 1 H by ... *here, why,* and *how.* If there is more ... swer first in your list of answers.

Listening Exercises ▲ 5

Note-Taking Skills

Making Better Sense of Your Notes

This activity will introduce you to a new note-taking system you might want to try. Now you might be thinking, "I've been taking notes for a long time, and have a system that works for me, why would I want to try something else?" Good question. But, I think I can answer it.

No matter how good your system of note taking might be, it can be improved. Also, the system below can help you: 1) recall more, 2) organize information more effectively, 3) focus on what you really need to know, and 4) save you a lot of time.

▶ Good reasons? If you agree that they are, take a few minutes right now and review the "Note-taking Skills" section in your handbook. Then read the instructions and tips below.

The Framework: Because every person learns a little differently, it is always good to try to fit any technique to your own learning style; the following framework provides opportunities for freedom of individual style.

Main Content	Notes to Myself

Main Content—In this section of your notes, you will write the main content or subject matter of the lecture. In a class setting, for example, this is the material you might be responsible for later on a test.

Note-Taking Tips: **Listen** carefully. **Think** about what is being said and always look for the "big picture." **Summarize** each main point in your own words. **Write** down what you need to remember, but listen more than you write.

Notes to Myself—In this section you can personalize your notes and interact with the content. Look for relationships, conclusions, questions. Write down personal thoughts, recollections, or memory devices.

Personal Tips: **Think** creatively. **Relate** the material to your own life whenever possible. **Develop** a system of abbreviations, symbols, mnemonic devices (Examples: ? for *"Ask a question about this"* or ★ for *"Key point, remember for the test"*). **Write** down questions or observations you want to think more about. **Review** your notes later and add more "notes to myself."

© Write Source, Box 460, Burlington, WI 53105   *Note-Taking Skills* ▲ 7

Using the Thesaurus

The *thesaurus* is a very useful reference book for writers of all ages. It offers students an incredible collection of synonyms and antonyms, all conveniently arranged in one book. But, as you'll soon see, a thesaurus offers much more help to writers than it first appears.

▶ READ the information in your handbook on the thesaurus. Then, after referring to the sample below, ANSWER THE QUESTIONS on using the index of the thesaurus.

369   INDEX   INCONSTANT

vicious **945**
IMPROPRIETY 24, 925
  [*see improper*]
improve **658**
  -the occasion 134
IMPROVEMENT **658**
improvident *careless* 460
  not preparing 674

inauspicious
  untimely 135
  untoward **830**
  adverse 512, 735
  hopeless 859
inborn *intrinsic* 5
  inbred **820**
inbound 294
incline *tend* 176

The Essay Test

The essay test is a very specific kind of writing. It requires a fairly formal writing style, since there is a very specific audience (your teacher) and a very specific purpose (to show your teacher that you know what you're talking about). So you see, writing an essay test is tricky business. Fortunately, the guidelines in your handbook can help you handle this very structured kind of writing.

▶ READ over the section in your handbook called "Guidelines for Taking an Essay Test." (Refer to "Essay, tests" in the index to find this information.) Then REWRITE the information given in to your own set of *eight guidelines.* We've given you the space to write below.

1. _____
2. _____
3. _____
4. _____
5. _____
6. _____
7. _____
8. _____

Psst! Right before you are to take an essay test, you should take a minute to breathe deeply and picture yourself doing well on the test. Envision yourself calm, in control, and writing competently. You can't be successful if you can't imagine it.

... ton, WI 53105

The Essay Test ▲ 13

▲ **10**

Building Vocabulary Skills
Using the Thesaurus
The Essay Test

◀ **11**

Note-Taking Skills
Listening Skills
Writing Directions

Practical Writing

Paragraph Writing **9**

Writing Business Letters **10** ▼

Writing Paragraphs

The **paragraph** is the workhorse of school writing. If you are able to write a good paragraph, you can easily learn to write a good essay, report, or essay test answer. Writing a good paragraph is really a matter of solving a problem. You won't always know when you begin writing how you can solve the problem—but you must know what the problem is. You must be able to state clearly at the very beginning what it is you are trying to do, what problem it is you are trying to solve. One way to do this is to use a **topic sentence** which contains both your subject and your feeling or impression about that subject.

▶ READ the opening page in the "Writing Paragraphs" section of your handbook and answer the questions below about paragraphs and topic sentences.

1. What is a paragraph—by definition? _____
_____

2. When is it a good idea to purposely compose a topic sentence for a paragraph?
_____
_____

3. When is it **not** a good idea to purposely compose a topic sentence for a paragraph?
_____
_____

▶ Next, READ the information on the "Topic Sentence" in your handbook and use what you've read to complete the statements below.

1. A topic sentence reveals what your subject is and _____

2. Here is a common formula for writing a topic sentence:
Formula: _____

Writing Business Letters

Why Write a Letter?

It doesn't really matter whether you use a computer, a telephone, a laser beam, or a letter to transfer your message: you are still the author of that message. But we all know that a telephone call is faster and more convenient than a letter, so why would anyone be concerned about knowing how to write a letter? Well, for one thing, faster and more convenient isn't always better. In the business world, for example, a letter has a number of very important advantages over just reaching out and touching somebody.

Psst! Remember why and under what circumstances you may want to write a business letter. Maybe you are going to be looking for a job or requesting information about a college program. Your handbook gives you specific advice about writing business letters for a variety of specific reasons.

▶ REFLECT: What advantages can you think of for writing a letter instead of making a phone call? Under what circumstances do you *need* to write letters? Have you ever written a business letter before? What were the circumstances? (Use the space below to record your thoughts or answer these questions.)

▶ READ about the advantages of letter writing in your handbook. Look up "The Advantages of a Written Message." (Refer to "LETTERS, Business" in the index.) Compare what you wrote above to what your handbook has to say. If your handbook discusses advantages you didn't think of, write those advantages in. Share the results of this reflect...

Writing on the Job

In-House Communications

A very mistaken idea exists among many students that once school is finished they will no longer have to worry about writing anything too important again. The truth is that writing (and reading, speaking, listening, computing, problem solving, etc.) will continue to be a very important part of most people's lives—and work—for a long time to come. (See article below.) Luckily, the assignments you are about to do are designed to help prepare you to handle just that kind of writing, the writing used most often "on the job."

An article in *Industry Week* (January 16, 1989, pp. 33-34) reported a recent survey of employers who cited 16 vital skills that workers need.

Knowing How to Learn: Rapidly changing business conditions demand employees who (1) know how to learn and use new information easily.

Competence: New technology requires (2) reading skills to understand it, (3) higher mathematical skills to use it, and (4) better writing skills to communicate about it.

Communication: (5) Listening and (6) speaking are the primary ways people communicate. Success on the job has been directly linked to communication skills.

Adaptability: Today's organizations give workers unprecedented responsibilities for decision making. Workers must have (7) creative thinking and (8) problem-solving skills to be able to make those decisions.

Personal Management: Individual workers' effectiveness is linked directly to (9) self-esteem, (10) goal setting and motivation, and (11) employability and career development.

Group Effectiveness: Dramatic changes in the workplace, including the tremendous increase in the use of workplace teams, have made (12) interpersonal skills, (13) negotiation, and (14) teamwork critical.

Influence: For (15) organization effectiveness, employees need a sense of the workings of a business and how their actions affect strategic goals. (16) Finally, leadership skills enable workers to understand and influence others.

© Write Source, Box 460, Burlington, WI 53105

Practical Writing ▲ 3

Letter of Application and Résumé

There's a lot you need to know about writing résumés and letters of application. It's important stuff—you'll need to know how to write these **well** if you expect to get any kind of job, let alone one you enjoy. And there are very few things more important than finding a job you can live with all day, five days a week.

Before we go on, you should know that there are two basic things you absolutely must do when writing a job application: You must be brief, and you must sell yourself. These things are harder to do than you might imagine. However, if you beat around the bush or if you're bashful, chances are someone else will get the job you wanted.

▶ Find out more by reading the handbook section called "The Letter of Application and Résumé." (Refer to "Résumé writing" in the index to find this information.) Then ANSWER the questions below.

What is the difference between a cover letter and an independent letter of application?
_____
_____
_____

What is a résumé? _____
_____

Name three things that are always included in a résumé:
_____
_____
_____

Why do you need to send a cover letter with a résumé?
_____
_____

What should you request in a cover letter?
_____
_____

AFTER • WORDS Get into small groups and discuss what you've read in this handbook section. Then talk about what types of jobs you are each planning to pursue after high school. How are you going to get these jobs? Who will you apply to? What skills do you have that make you suited to the jobs you want to get? Treat this discussion as an informal preliminary to job hunting. Sometimes talking your plans over with someone can help clarify those plans and create enthusiasm.

© Write Source, Box 460, Burlington, WI 53105

Practical Writing ▲ 3

▲

11 Writing on the Job

12 Letter of Application & Résumé

Writing Across the Curriculum

Writing "Assignments" in the Content Areas

Designing Your Own Assignments

SUBJECT:

AUDIENCE:

Writing Across the Curriculum

Teaching with Writing . . .

Journal writing, dialogues, stories, and letters—these popular forms of writing have traditionally been associated exclusively with the language arts curriculum. But not any longer. There are more and more teachers across the curriculum who have their students explore their thoughts and feelings in journals, confront challenging ideas in dialogues, and develop historical and scientific stories. And why so?

These teachers realize that writing plays a central role in the learning process. Writing by its very nature gets students actively and thoughtfully involved in their work no matter if they are studying algebraic equations, photosynthesis, or local government. It helps them understand and remember important concepts. It makes them more appreciative of course content, and curious to learn more. And it gives them control over their own learning. (Not

become or remain active and interested learners. Without this proficiency, it is next to impossible for students to succeed in any content area. How can students display any level of mastery in social studies, for instance, if they can't write, read, or talk about it?

Some experts would say that writing and reading (as well as the other language arts) should be a primary focus of instruction across the curriculum. So many of the abilities we want to instill in students stem from language proficiency: to be responsive and critical thinkers, to be effective and accurate communicators, and to be resourceful and purposeful readers.

What We Have in Mind

The level of literacy we have in mind can't be achieved unless all teachers in all content areas do their parts. Language proficiency de-

---

Writing "Assignments"

What follows are ideas for writing assignments arranged according to content area. A suggested grade level is also indicated in parentheses. The category of "Field Studies" is included with ideas for many technical, fine arts, or applied arts topics.

Special Note: With a few adjustments many of the ideas listed here will work in more than one content area and in more than one grade level. Individual teachers or teams will ultimately decide where each idea best fits the needs or nature of students.

■ **SCIENCE**

Bridges to Physics

Writing Framework Record

	SELECTING	COLLECTING	WRITING	REVISING	PROOFING	PUBLISHING
PERSONAL WRITING						
Reminiscence of a Person						
"Unpeopled" Reminiscence						
SUBJECT WRITING						
Description of a Place						
Interview Report						
Report of Firsthand Experience						
Compiled Report from Multiple Interviews						
CREATIVE WRITING						
Fictionalized Memory						
Patterned Fiction						

Assessing Your Students' Work

The *Writers File* provides a wide variety of language experiences for students. They have opportunities to immerse themselves in personal, subject, creative, reflective, and academic writing; to learn about each phase of the writing process in the many workshops and minilessons; and to improve their basic writing and study skills in the language and resource folder materials. The information that follows will help you and your students evaluate their progress in the series.

How should I assess my students' performance in the *Writers File*?

The purpose of each activity in the *Writers File* is to give students a stimulating and meaningful language-learning experience. Few, if any, of the activities can or should be judged in terms of right or wrong answers. The best methods of assessment for the work in the series are the authentic approaches common in many language arts classrooms today, especially those that are outcome- or performance-based (portfolios, for example). Although the details of these approaches vary from school to school, they share several important characteristics:

■ They are practical and functional for both students and teachers.

■ They are flexible and easy to individualize.

■ They incorporate assessments at every stage in the writing process.

■ They include assessments by the writer, the teacher, and peers.

■ They encourage assessments which are positive and constructive.

> *"If any man wishes to write in a clear style, let him first be clear in his thoughts."*
> – Johann Wolfgang von Goethe

What are the best methods for assessing my students' writing?

Two kinds of evaluation interest teachers today: **formative** (evaluating while the student is "forming" the project) and **summative** (evaluating the total outcome, or sum, of the student's effort). Formative evaluation does not result in a grade; summative evaluation does. Some teachers do choose, however, to give students a set number of points during different stages in the formative steps in the writing process.

FORMATIVE EVALUATION

Formative evaluation is most often used for writing-to-learn activities, prewriting activities, writing in progress, journal entries, and so forth. Four types of formative evaluation are widely used:

■ Desk-side conferences
■ Scheduled teacher/student conferences
■ Written questions and responses
■ Peer responses

DESK-SIDE CONFERENCES occur when a teacher stops at a student's desk to ask questions and make responses while students are working. In the early stages of the writing process, responses and questions should be about writing ideas, content, audience, purpose, generating ideas, and getting those ideas on paper. Questions should be open-ended. This gives the writer "space" to talk. When a writer is talking, she or he is thinking, clarifying, and making decisions. Teachers should not attempt to solve problems for the students, but instead ask questions and suggest possible solutions.

Hint Respond to a student's paper as a reader, not a teacher. Address "under development," the most common problem young writers face in the first stages of the writing process. Also see the PQS conference format discussed on the next page.

Setting Up a Writing Workshop

Performance-Based Evaluation

One way to evaluate student performance is to set up a clear set of guidelines and a grading scale for the entire quarter or semester. These guidelines should spell out clearly the kind of work expected of each student in terms of both quality and quantity; the grading scale should be equally clear.

One Classroom Model

The sample which follows has been used very successfully over the past 15 years in a sophomore writing course. Each student in the class worked out an individual course of study based on previous performance, past teacher recommendations, a written pretest, and a teacher-student conference. (See the "Individualized Writing Framework" on p. 10.) The teacher decided which 18 (more or less) writing assignments would be included—and in what order—and then met with each student. The objective was to find a starting point that was appropriate for each individual student.

Student assessment was based on performance (successful completion of a predetermined number of writing and language activities). A point system was used to keep track of student performance, one which encouraged individualization based on student needs. (See the summary of that point system in the right-hand column.)

Adjusting the Scale

As you will see, students were required to complete a number of writing workshops, journal entries (see p. 11), classroom sharings, peer editing sessions, and other activities in addition to the writing "framework" assignments.

Note: As you might expect, this scale has been altered many times over the past 15 years. You would most likely alter it as well so that it works for you and your students. If, for example, your performance-based courses are set up with an A, B, I scale, students simply receive *Incompletes* until they had accumulate 170 points.

POINT SYSTEM

Quarter/Semester		Grade
100	200	A+
95	190	A
93	186	A-
91	182	B+
88	176	B
85	170	B-
83	166	C+
80	160	C
77	154	C-
75	150	D+
73	146	D
70	140	D-
Less than 70	140	F (I)

1. Successful completion of each of the seven major **writing assignments** (framework activities) is worth 15 points. (Total points possible: 105)

> *Please note:* Eight points will be given for an assignment not completed but beyond the rough draft stage at the time the grading period ends.

2. Successful completion of each of the 15 assigned **writing workshops** is worth 2 points each. (Total possible: 30)

3. Each outside **journal entry** is worth 1 point. (Total possible: 20)

4. Each **classroom sharing** of a journal entry is also worth 1 point. (Total possible: 15)

5. Each of the required 10 **peer editing** sheets is worth 2 points each. (Total possible: 20)

6. **Additional points** can also be earned for doing additional workshops or peer editing sheets, as well as for submitting a finished piece for publication. (Total possible: 10)

Assessing & Monitoring

Responding to Student Writing

Using Writing Portfolios

Setting Up a Writing Workshop

Monitoring Writing Workshops

Recommended Books and Materials

Coordinating *Writers INC* Material

The *Writers File* for 9, 10, 11, and 12

The *Writers File* provides a "sequence" of reproducible writing and language activities for levels 9, 10, 11, and 12. The *Writers File* can serve as the focus of a new and stimulating writing program when used with the *Writers INC* handbook, or it can supplement an existing program. Each level in the series is made up of 18 "sequential" writing activities, 40 writing workshops, over 200 daily language activities, and numerous forms, strategies, and other resources. Together they provide a program that is not only comprehensive, but cost-effective. (All activities are reproducible and come conveniently arranged in a three-ring binder.)

Student Folders

Laminated, heavy-duty pocket folders are punched for use in three-ring binders.

■ **Topic Folders** are printed with over 150 topics for free writing. They also contain an easy-to-use chart which allows students to keep track of their writing progress.

■ **Punctuation Pockets** will answer anyone's punctuation and capitalization questions. A complete list of rules is printed on the inside and outside of this folder.

■ **Writing Folder** provides guidelines and advice before, during, and after the writing process. Each folder can also serve as a "portfolio" for work-in-progress as well as completed writing.

Personal Writing Books

Write in here is a "blank" personal writing book just waiting to be filled with thoughts and feelings. Use for free writing and journals, final drafts, and personal anthologies, early efforts, and polished gems. *Write in here* also contains a list of free-writing topics and a writing-progress chart.

Reflections stimulates and challenges students with thought-provoking ideas, quotations, and photos. *A Daily Journal* and the *Reader Response Journal* contain suggestions on keeping a journal and plenty of space to begin.

**Write Source Educational Publishing House
Box 460, Burlington, WI 53105
Phone 1-800-445-8613 • Fax 1-414-763-2651**

Professional Titles for High-School Teachers and Students

The Write Source Educational Publishing House highly recommends the following titles on writing and teaching for high-school teachers, coordinators, and administrators.

Note: All of these titles are available through Heinemann-Boynton/Cook unless indicated otherwise.

Active Voice: A Writing Program Across the Curriculum — James Moffett

Active Voice includes Moffett's latest recommendations for writing assignments and writing-group management. The assignments in *Active Voice* are designed to be repeated with variations throughout a writer's schooling.

Beat Not the Poor Desk — Marie Ponsot and Rosemary Deen

Winner of the 1982 Mina P. Saughnessy Prize, *Beat Not* offers a revolutionary inductive approach to teaching composition, in particular the essay. As stimulating to the instructor as to the student, this book helps students develop elemental skills by the incremental repetition of integrated writing assignments. *Beat Not* also offers a rationale for a year's worth of writing assignments.

The I-Search Paper — James Macrorie

The I-Search Paper is more than a textbook; it is a new form of instructional guide—a *context* book—that invites students to join the author and teacher in the new educational movement called "Writing to Learn." To put this book in the hands of all students will help them carry out active, meaningful, and stimulating research projects.

In the Middle — Nancie Atwell

Ms. Atwell details her successful writing and reading workshops in *In the Middle*. It contains a clear discussion of workshop procedures, practical advice, techniques for conferring with writers and readers, and many examples of student writing. All teachers of writing and reading should share in Ms. Atwell's experiences.

Inside Out — Dan Kirby and Tim Liner

Kirby and Liner share their best strategies for teaching writing and enjoying the experience. *Inside Out* contains suggestions for writing assignments, classroom management, and teaching methods. All of the ideas, which are presented in a sincere and friendly manner, promote thinking and learning through writing.

Learning to Write/Writing to Learn — John S. Mayher, Nancy Lester, Gordon M. Pradl

Based on the CBS-TV Sunrise Semester programs, *Learning to Write* draws on the authors' experiences with in-service programs across the country. Many of the practical ideas have been used by teachers in grades K-12 in schools currently implementing writing across the curriculum programs.

Mind Matters — Dan Kirby and Carol Kuyendall

Mind Matters seeks to help teachers sort through the body of research into the workings of the mind and apply these insights in the thinking and learning that goes on, or should go on, in their classrooms. *Mind Matters* is directed primarily at teachers to serve as a resource of ideas and background information.

Portfolios: Process and Product — Pat Belanoff and Marcia Dickson, editors

Portfolios, the first book to focus exclusively on portfolio assessment, is both practical and theoretical, offering places to start rather than claiming to be definitive. The articles, all written by teachers with experience in using portfolio grading, are free of jargon, making sound composition and assessment theory available to every reader, regardless of grade level. Some of the articles describe possible pitfalls in planning strategies and offer suggestions for avoiding them.

Roots in the Sawdust: Writing to Learn Across the Disciplines — Anne Ruggles Gere, etc. (An NCTE publication)

Using the metaphor of the nurse log, the fallen tree that provides a foundation for many varied plants, this book is useful for all parts of the educational system: administrators will make their schools more effective through the incorporation of its writing-to-learn techniques; students will become active learners; and teachers will see improved student learning without adding to already burdensome grading loads.

Recommended Reading: Crate Books

Classic & Modern Literature

SET 1 - Highly Recommended for College Bound

GRADE LEVEL 9

All Quiet on the
  Western Front .... Remarque
Black Like Me .... Griffin
Frankenstein .... Shelley
The Good Earth .... Buck
Great Expectations .... Dickens
Great Tales and Poems of
  Edgar Allen Poe .... Poe
The Heart Is a Lonely Hunter .... McCullers
Hound of the Baskervilles .... Doyle
The Iliad .... Homer (Rouse)
Life on the Mississippi .... Twain
The Little Prince .... Saint Exupery
Lord of the Flies .... Golding
The Odyssey .... Homer (Rouse)
Oliver Twist .... Dickens
The Once and Future King .... White
Oregon Trail .... Parkman
Ox-Bow Incident .... Clark
Reader's Companion to
  World Literature .... Horstein, et al.
A Separate Peace .... Knowles
The Three Musketeers .... Dumas
To Kill a Mockingbird .... Lee
Order No. 4013

SET 2 - Enrichment for College Bound

GRADE LEVEL 9

Autobiography of Miss
  Jane Pittman .... Gaines
The Chosen .... Potok
David Copperfield .... Dickens
Death Be Not Proud .... Gunther
Effect of Gamma Rays on Man-in-
  the-Moon Marigolds .... Zindel
Go Tell It on the Mountain .... Baldwin
I Know Why the Caged
  Bird Sings .... Angelou
Lost Horizon .... Hilton
My Antonia .... Cather
Mythology .... Hamilton
Profiles in Courage .... Kennedy
Pudd'nhead Wilson .... Twain
Raisin in the Sun .... Hansberry
Romeo and Juliet and West
  Side Story .... Shakespeare/Shulman
Roots .... Haley
Silas Marner .... Eliot
21 Great Stories .... Lass & Tasman, eds.
Up From Slavery .... Washington
When the Legends Die .... Borland
The Yearling .... Rawlings
Order No. 4014

Popular Literature

GRADE LEVEL 9

Beyond the Chocolate War .... Cormier
The Bloody Country .... Collier
Circle of Children .... MacCracken
Cold Sassy Tree .... Burns
The Contender .... Lipsyte
Dibs in Search of Self .... Axline
Durango Street.................................. Bonham
Flowers for Algernon .... Keyes
I Am the Cheese .... Cormier
I Never Loved Your Mind .... Zindel
I Never Promised You
  a Rose Garden .... Greenberg
Lovey: A Very Special
  Child .... MacCracken
Mr. & Mrs. Bo Jo Jones .... Head
Night .... Wiesel
A Night to Remember .... Lord
Rainbow Jordan .... Childress
Something Wicked This Way
  Comes .... Bradbury
Watership Down .... Adams
The Wave... Strasser
Wolf Rider.. Avi
Order No. 4015

Classic American Literature

SET 1 - Highly Recommended for College Bound

GRADE LEVELS 10 & 11

The Adventures of
  Huckleberry Finn .... Twain
American Short
  Story, Vol. 1 .... Skaggs, ed.
American Short
  Story, Vol. 2 .... Skaggs, ed.
Auto. and Other Writings .... Franklin
Babbitt .... Lewis
Billy Budd .... Melville
For Whom the Bell Tolls .... Hemingway
Grapes of Wrath .... Steinbeck
The Great Gatsby .... Fitzgerald
House of Seven Gables .... Hawthorne
Intruder in the Dust .... Faulkner
The Jungle .... Sinclair
Last of the Mohicans .... Cooper
Main Street .... Lewis
Moby Dick....................................... Melville
Of Mice and Men .... Steinbeck
Our Town .... Wilder
The Scarlet Letter .... Hawthorne
Walden and Other Writings .... Thoreau
Order No. 4016

Classic American Literature

SET 2 — Enrichment for College Bound

GRADE LEVELS 10 & 11

Celestial Railroad and
  Other Stories .... Hawthorne
A Connecticut Yankee in
  King Arthur's Court .... Twain
A Death in the Family .... Agee
Death of a Salesman .... Miller
Ethan Frome .... Wharton
The Fixer .... Malamud
Giants in the Earth .... Rolvaag
The Human Comedy .... Saroyan
Invisible Man .... Ellison
The Major American
  Poets .... Williams & Honig, eds.
Narrative of the Life of
  Frederick Douglass .... Douglass
Rabbit Run .... Updike
The Sound and the Fury .... Faulkner
The Sun Also Rises .... Hemingway
Tender Is the Night .... Fitzgerald
Three by Tennessee .... Williams
Travels with Charley .... Steinbeck
Winesburg, Ohio .... Anderson
Order No. 4017

Popular Literature

GRADE LEVEL 10

About David .... Pfeffer
Alive .... Read
Bless the Beasts and
  Children .... Swarthout
The Butterfly Revolution .... Butler
Chinese Handcuffs .... Crutcher
Dibs in Search of Self .... Axline
Dune .... Herbert
Firestarter .... King
Gandhi: His Life
  and Message .... Fischer
Growing Up .... Baker
Guns of Navarone .... MacLean
Hobbit.. Tolkien
I Heard the Owl Call
  My Name .... Craven
Lord of the Flies .... Golding
Member of the Wedding .... McCullers
Murder on the Orient Express .... Christie
The Pigman .... Zindel
The Pigman's Legacy .... Zindel
Return of the King .... Tolkien
75 Short Masterpieces .... Goodman, ed.
Order No. 4018

College instructors agree that college-bound students should read in and of the classics. That is why we offer an extensive list of classic titles. Instructors agree as well that these student should supplement their reading of the classics with a wide range of important literary works. That is why we offer an extensive list of important modern titles, drama and short story collections, and biographies. Instructors also feel it is important for students to develop a genuine interest in reading. That is why we offer a substantial list of popular young adult titles.

We've developed sets of Crate Books based on the above recommendations. We offer one crate of classic and important modern titles appropriate for each grade level. A second enrichment crate offers a wide range of additional important titles. A third crate offers popular high-interest titles. Used together, these sets of books provide a perfect classroom library for your college-bound students.

■ Call for current prices.

English & Irish Lit.

SET 1 - Highly Recommended for **College Bound**

GRADE LEVELS 10 & 11

Animal Farm .... Orwell
Beowulf .... Raffel, trans.
Brave New World .... Huxley
Canterbury Tales .... Chaucer
Emma .... Austen
Gulliver's Travels .... Swift
Jane Eyre .... Bronte
Lord Jim .... Conrad
The Major British Poets .... Williams, ed.
1984 .... Orwell
Portrait of the Artist .... Joyce
Pride and Prejudice .... Austen
Pygmalion .... Shaw
Return of the Native .... Hardy
Tale of Two Cities .... Dickens
The Turn of the Screw .... James
Utopia .... More
Vanity Fair .... Thackeray
Wuthering Heights .... Bronte

Order No. 4019

SET 2 - **Recommended for College-Bound Seminars/Individual Study**

GRADE LEVELS 10 & 11

Doctor Faustus .... Marlowe
The Elephant Man............................. Sparks
Heart of Darkness and
   The Secret Sharer .... Conrad
Idylls of the King and
   a Selection of Poems .... Tennyson
Joseph Andrews .... Fielding
Le Morte D'Arthur .... Malory
A Man for All Seasons .... Bolt
The Mayor of Casterbridge................. Hardy
Paradise Lost .... Milton
The Picture of Dorian Gray .... Wilde
Pilgrim's Progress .... Bunyan
The Portrait of a Lady .... James
The Power and the Glory .... Greene
Saint Joan .... Shaw
Signet Classic Book of British
   Short Stories .... Karl, ed.
Tess of d'Urbervilles .... Hardy
Tom Jones .... Fielding
Vicar of Wakefield .... Goldsmith

Order No. 4020

Popular Literature

GRADE LEVEL 11

The Bell Jar .... Plath
Christine .... King
Christy .... Marshall
Day of Infamy .... Lord
Fail-Safe .... Burdick/Wheeler
The Fellowship of the Ring .... Tolkien
15 Amer. One-Act Plays .... Kozelka, ed.
Go Ask Alice .... Anonymous
Homecoming .... Voigt
I Know Why the Caged
   Bird Sings .... Angelou
I Never Promised You
   a Rose Garden .... Greenberg
I'm OK, You're OK .... Harris
In Cold Blood .... Capote
The Loneliness of the Long-
   Distance Runner .... Sillitoe
Manchild in the Promised Land .... Brown
The Natural .... Malamud
No Language But a Cry .... D'Ambrosio
Points of View .... Moffet/McElheny
Welcome to Monkey House.......... Vonnegut

Order No. 4021

Classic World Literature

SET 1 - Highly Recommended for **College Bound**

GRADE LEVEL 12

The Aeneid .... Vergil
Anna Karenina .... Tolstoy
Candide and Zadig and
   Selected Stories .... Voltaire
Chekhov: The Major Plays .... Chekhov
Crime and Punishment .... Dostoyevsky
Cry, the Beloved Country .... Paton
Cyrano de Bergerac .... Rostond
A Doll's House .... Ibsen
Don Quixote .... Cervantes
Great Dialogues of Plato .... Plato
The Hunchback of Notre Dame .... Hugo
The Idiot .... Dostoyevsky
Madame Bovary .... Flaubert
One Day in the Life
   of Ivan Denisovich .... Solzhenitsyn
The Plague .... Camus
Three Theban Plays .... Sophocles

Order No. 4022

Classic World Literature

SET 2 - Enrichment for College Bound

GRADE LEVEL 12

The Brothers Karamazov .... Dostoyevsky
The Death of Ivan Ilych .... Tolstoy
Eight Great Comedies
   .... Barnet, Berman, and Burto
Eight Great Tragedies
   .... Barnet, Berman, and Burto
Fathers and Sons .... Turgenev
Ghandi: His Life and Message .... Fischer
The Inferno .... Dante
Metamorphosis .... Kafka
No Exit and Other Plays .... Sartre
Notes from the Underground
   and Other Stories .... Dostoyevsky
Orestes Plays of
   Aeschylus .... Aeschylus
The Prince .... Machiavelli
The Stranger .... Camus
Three Great Plays
   of Euripides .... Euripedes
Waiting for Godot .... Beckett
War and Peace .... Tolstoy

Order No. 4023

Popular Literature

GRADE LEVEL 12

As I Lay Dying .... Faulkner
Being There .... Kosinski
Cannery Row .... Steinbeck
Catch 22 .... Heller
A Clockwork Orange .... Burgess
Coming of Age in Mississippi .... Moody
Deliverance .... Dickey
Electric Kool-Aid Acid Test .... Wolfe
The Elephant Man............................. Sparks
The Fountainhead .... Rand
Future Shock .... Toffler
Great British Dectective .... Goulart, ed.
Native Son .... Wright
One Flew Over the
   Cuckoo's Nest .... Kesey
Slaughterhouse Five .... Vonnegut
2001: A Space Odyssey .... Clarke
Two Towers .... Tolkein
Who's Afraid of Virginia Woolf .... Albee

Order No. 4024

How does the *Writers INC Language Series* compare with a traditional textbook series?

When **more** is less . . .

The *Writers INC Series* actually does offer more for less. Rather than a textbook which contains both instruction and activities, the handbook provides information, inspiration, and guidelines—but no activities. (The *Writers File* activities are separate and can be used at the teacher's discretion.) This makes it possible for students to carry valuable writing-related information with them wherever they go. As we know, writing doesn't just happen in the language classroom—it's an all-school, all-day activity.

See for yourself how much more the *Writers INC Language Series* offers you and your students and how little it costs compared to a traditional textbook series.

Traditional Textbook Series	Writers INC Series
❑ **predetermined sequence** . . . assumes that a writing and language program should be built around a predetermined sequence of activities located within a series of textbooks	■ **flexible sequence** . . . recognizes that students learn best when they use their own ideas and write for real audiences; students and teachers determine the language sequence
❑ **expansive text** . . . begins and ends with oversized texts that are seen by students as imposing and impersonal	■ **portable resource** . . . offers a 378-page handbook of portable, useful information which students can refer to in the language classroom and across the curriculum
❑ **traditional approach** . . . customarily addresses students in a formal tone and places a great deal of attention on isolated skills work	■ **personalized approach** . . . speaks in a friendly, reassuring voice that engages students in the explanations, guidelines, and examples
❑ **classwide instruction** . . . usually prescribes that units or chapters be taught to all students at the same time	■ **individual needs** . . . provides a flexible program of activities to better meet individual teaching styles and student needs
❑ **language classroom** . . . focuses almost exclusively on writing in the language classroom	■ **across the curriculum** . . . encourages writing, thinking, and learning in all content areas
❑ **teacher-centered** . . . is dependent on teacher instruction	■ **student-centered** . . . encourages self-improvement and independent learning
❑ **costly** . . . can be very costly	■ **cost-effective** . . . is very cost-effective

tape here (also tape the sides if you've enclosed a check)

place
stamp
here

Write Source
Educational Publishing House
P.O. Box 460
Burlington, WI 53105

Building a Schoolwide Writing Program with the *Writers INC Language Series*

More and more, high-school teachers want a writing and language program that is flexible and multifaceted, a foundation to build on without tying a school district to a costly textbook series for years to come. With the *Writers INC* handbook and teacher's guide, plus the *Writers File* activities, teachers have that foundation and more.

The *Writers File* for 9, 10, 11, and 12

The *Writers File* provides a "sequence" of reproducible writing and language activities for levels 9, 10, 11, and 12. The *Writers File* can serve as the focus of a new and stimulating writing program when used with the *Writers INC* handbook, or it can supplement an existing program. Each level in the series is made up of 18 "sequential" writing activities, 50-60 writing workshops, over 200 daily language activities, and numerous forms, strategies, and other resources. Together they provide a program that is not only comprehensive, but very cost-effective. (All activities are reproducible and come conveniently arranged in a three-ring binder.)

Separate activity "Files" are available for grades 9-12.

Cat. Number	Quantity	Title	List Price	*School Price	25 or more	Total
0081		***Writers INC*** (softcover)	9.95	**7.95**	**7.50**	
0082		***Writers INC*** (hardcover)	12.95	**9.95**	**9.50**	
0039		***INC Sights*** (teacher's guide)	12.95	**9.95**	**9.50**	
0109		**Level 9 – *Writers File***	129.95	**99.95**		
0110		**Level 10 – *Writers File***	129.95	**99.95**		
0111		**Level 11 – *Writers File***	129.95	**99.95**		
0112		**Level 12 – *Writers File***	129.95	**99.95**		

☐ **Check**   ☐ **MasterCard**   ☐ **Visa**

Card Number _____ Expiration Date _____

Signature (Required for credit card purchases) _____

Subtotal _____
Shipping ADD 8% _____
(Wis. Residents ADD 5%) _____
GRAND TOTAL _____

(*Prices good through Dec. 31, 1993)

BILL TO: **P.O. No.**

School

Purchased by

Address

City   State   ZIP

SHIP TO: **Phone**

School

Attention

School Address

City   State   ZIP

To order by phone call 1-800-445-8613; by fax 1-414-763-2651.

Index